HANDBOOK OF ANTHROPOLOGY

HANDBOOK OF ANTHROPOLOGY

Krishnanand Sanwal

AKANSHA PUBLISHING HOUSE
NEW DELHI - 110 002 (INDIA)

AKANSHA PUBLISHING HOUSE
4649/21-B, Ansari Road
Daryaganj, New Delhi - 110 002
Phones: 23263193, 9811582579
E-mail: ektabooks@yahoo.com

Handbook of Anthropology

First Published, 2007

ISBN 978-81-8370-122-8

PRINTED IN INDIA

Published by Akansha Publishing House, New Delhi - 110 002 and Printed at Capital Offset Press, Delhi

To

Professor LP Vidyarthi

the doyen of Anthropology

in India

CONTENTS

PREFACE

> "The difference between a river and a swamp is that a river is confined within banks, while a swamp is not... Because a river is confined, and channeled, it has life. It is a mighty, moving, living thing. Because a swamp has no restrictions, it becomes thin and stagnant. ... In our modern life we boast of freedom. We want life without restrictions and without confinement. Only we forget that such living becomes stagnant."
>
> —*Leonard Cochran*

Anthropology can best be understood as an outgrowth of the Age of Enlightenment, a period when Europeans attempted systematically to study human behavior, the known varieties of which had been increasing since the 15th century as a result of the First European colonization wave. The traditions of jurisprudence, history, philology, and sociology then evolved into something more closely resembling the modern views of these disciplines and informed the development of the social sciences, of which anthropology was a part.

In the words of Eric Wolf. anthropology is "the most scientific of the humanities, and the most humanistic of the sciences." Contemporary anthropologists claim a number of earlier thinkers as their forebears, and the discipline has several sources; Claude Lévi-Strauss, for example, claimed Montaigne and Rousseau as important influences. The Romantic reaction to the Enlightenment produced thinkers, such as Johann Gottfried Herder and later Wilhelm Dilthey, whose work formed the basis for the "culture concept," which is central to the study of anthropology.

It is remarkable to note that institutionally, anthropology emerged from the development of natural history that occurred during the European colonization of the 17th, 18th, 19th and 20th centuries. Programmes of ethnographic study originated in this era as the study of the "human primitives" overseen by colonial administrations. There was a tendency in late 18th century Enlightenment thought to understand human society as natural phenomena that behaved in accordance with certain principles and that could be observed empirically. In some ways, studying the language, culture, physiology, and artifacts of European colonies was not unlike studying the flora and fauna of those places.

As academic disciplines began to differentiate over the course of the 19th century, anthropology grew increasingly distinct from natural history, on the one hand, and from purely historical or literary fields such as Classics, on the other. A common criticism has been that other fields focus disproportionately on the Westerns while anthropology focuses disproportionately on "others".

As a significant development, in the twentieth century, academic disciplines have often been institutionally divided into three broad domains. The natural and biological sciences seek to derive general laws through reproducible and falsifiable experiments. The humanities generally study different local traditions, through their history, literature, music, and arts, with an emphasis on understanding particular individuals, events, or eras. The *social sciences* have generally attempted to develop scientific methods to understand social phenomena in a generalizable way, though usually with methods distinct from those of the natural sciences. In particular, social sciences often develop statistical descriptions rather than the general laws derived in physics or chemistry, or they may explain individual cases through more general principles, as in many fields of psychology. Obviously, Anthropology does not easily fit into one of these categories, and different branches of anthropology draw on one or more of these domains.

Anthropology as it emerged among the colonial powers has generally taken a different path than that in the countries of southern and central Europe (Italy, Greece, and the successors to the Austro-Hungarian and Ottoman empires). In the former, the encounter with multiple, distinct cultures, often very different in organization and language from those of Europe, has led to a continuing emphasis on cross-cultural comparison and a receptiveness to certain kinds of cultural relativism. In the successor states of continental Europe, on the other hand, anthropologists often joined with folklorists and linguists in the nationalist/nation-building enterprise.

Ethnologists in these countries tended to focus on differentiating among local ethnolinguistic groups, documenting local folk culture, and representing the prehistory of the nation through museums and other forms of public education. In this scheme, Russia occupied a middle position. On the one hand, it had a large Asian region of highly distinct, pre-industrial, often non-literate peoples, similar to the situation in the Americas; on the other hand, Russia also participated to some degree in the nationalist discourses of Central and Eastern Europe. After the Revolution of 1917, anthropology in the USSR and later the Soviet Bloc countries were highly shaped by the need to conform to Marxist theories of social evolution.

Admist the plenty of literature, this book is unique. As is obvious from the name of the title, an endeavour is made here in this book to bring together all relevant material to describe anthropolgy in composite and coherent manner. After defining the main concepts and inherent theories, all major branches with subfields of the discipline are given an elaborate treatment.

The following chapters make core of the study: Introduction to Anthropology; Evolution of Human Being; Philosophical & Theological Anthropology; Social Anthropology; Cultural Anthropology; Physical (Biological) Anthropology; Tribals (Adivasis) of India; Sociolinguistics and Anthropology: Structural Analysis & Ethics in Anthropology etc. Prominent men of letters who have founded and contributed significantly to the development of the discipline are listed in an appendix. Besides this, glossary of terms is an added feature of the book.

Expectedly, this will prove an ideal text-cum-reference book to students, researchers and teachers besides the aspirants appearing for various competitive examinations.

In fact, the work of this nature cannot be materialised without drawing upon the works/ideas of experts in the field. We have taken help from various authoritative source e.g. books, articles, monographs, reports etc., penned by leading scholars.

We express our gratitude to them all. Every efforts is made to acknowledge the original contributors, if someone missed inadevertently, we owe a deep sense of gratitude to them also. We are equally grateful to our teachers, friends and colleagues for their inspiration, constant moral support, guidance and assistance.

Finally, the publisher deserves our all appreciation for bringing out this book in superb way.

Further, constructive criticism and suggestions are welcome from all quarters to improve the utility of this by making it more informative.

—KS

INTRODUCTION TO ANTHROPOLOGY

> "Of all the vanities and fopperies, the vanity of high birth is the greatest. True nobility is derived from virtue, not from birth. Titles, indeed, may be purchased, but virtue is the only coin that makes the bargain valid."
>
> —*Robert Burton*

The term Anthropology is derived from Greek *anthropos* meaning human being and *logos* i.e. knowledge, which is the holistic study of humanity. Anthropology has origins in the natural sciences, the humanities, and the social sciences. Ethnography is both one its primary methods, and the text that is written as a result of the practice of anthropology.

It must be remembered that since the work of Franz Boas and Bronisiaw Malinowski in the late 19th- and early 20th-centuries, cultural and social anthropology has been distinguished from other social science disciplines by its emphasis on in-depth examination of context, cross-cultural comparisons (socio-cultural anthropology is by nature a comparative discipline), and the importance it places on long-term, experiential immersion in the area of research, often known as participant-observation. Cultural-Social anthropology in particular has emphasized cultural relativity and the use of their findings to frame cultural critiques.

This has been particularly prominent in America, from Boas's arguments against 19th-century racial ideology, through Margaret Mead's advocacy for gender equality and sexual liberation, to current criticisms of post-colonial oppression and promotion of multiculturalism.

The renowned anthropologist Eric Wolf has described anthropology as "the most scientific of the humanities, and the most humanistic of the sciences." Contemporary anthropologists claim a number of earlier thinkers as their forebears, and the discipline has several sources; Claude Lévi-Strauss, for example, claimed Montaigne and Rousseau as important influences. Anthropology can best be understood as an outgrowth of the Age of Enlightenment, a period when Europeans attempted systematically to study human behavior, the known varieties of which had been increasing since the 15th century as a result of the First European colonization wave. The traditions of jurisprudence, history, philology, and sociology then evolved into something more closely resembling the modern views of these disciplines and informed the development of the social sciences, of which anthropology was a part. At the same time, the Romantic reaction to the Enlightenment produced thinkers, such as Johann Gottfried Herder and later Wilhelm Dilthey, whose work formed the basis for the "culture concept," which is central to the study of anthropology.

It is remarkable to note that institutionally, anthropology emerged from the development of natural history (expounded by authors such as Buffon) that occurred during the European colonization of the 17th, 18th, 19th and 20th centuries. Programs of ethnographic study originated in this era as the study of the "human primitives" overseen by colonial administrations. There was a tendency in late 18th century Enlightenment thought to understand human society as natural phenomena that behaved in accordance with certain principles and that could be observed empirically. In some ways, studying the language, culture, physiology, and artifacts of European colonies was not unlike studying the flora and fauna of those places.

Notably, early anthropology was divided between proponents of unilinealism, who argued that all societies passed through a single evolutionary process, from the most primitive to the most advanced, and various forms of non-lineal theorists, who tended to subscribe to ideas such as diffusionism. Most 19th-century social theorists, including anthropologists, viewed non-European societies as windows onto the pre-industrial human past. As academic disciplines began to differentiate over the course of the 19th century, anthropology grew increasingly distinct from natural history, on the one hand, and from purely historical or literary fields such as Classics, on the other. A common criticism has been that other fields focus disproportionately on the Westerns while anthropology focuses disproportionately on "others".

As a significant development, in the twentieth century, academic disciplines have often been institutionally divided into three broad domains. The natural and biological *sciences* seek to derive general laws through reproducible and falsifiable experiments. The *humanities* generally study different local traditions, through their history, literature, music, and arts, with an emphasis on understanding particular individuals, events, or eras. The *social sciences* have generally attempted to develop scientific methods to understand social phenomena in a generalizable way, though usually with methods distinct from those of the natural sciences. In particular, social sciences often develop statistical descriptions rather than the general laws derived in physics or chemistry, or they may explain individual cases through more general principles, as in many fields of psychology. Anthropology (like some fields of history) does not easily fit into one of these categories, and different branches of anthropology draw on one or more of these domains.

Anthropology as it emerged among the colonial powers has generally taken a different path than that in the countries of southern and central Europe (Italy, Greece, and the successors to the Austro-Hungarian and Ottoman empires). In the former, the encounter with multiple, distinct cultures, often very different in organization and language from those of Europe, has led to a continuing emphasis on cross-cultural comparison and a receptiveness to certain kinds of cultural relativism. In the successor states of continental Europe, on the other hand, anthropologists often joined with folklorists and linguists in the nationalist/nation-building enterprise. Ethnologists in these countries tended to focus on differentiating among local ethnolinguistic groups, documenting local folk culture, and representing the prehistory of the nation through museums and other forms of public education. In this scheme, Russia occupied a middle position. On the one hand, it had a large Asian region of highly distinct, pre-industrial, often non-literate peoples, similar to the situation in the Americas; on the other hand, Russia also participated to some degree in the nationalist discourses of Central and Eastern Europe. After the Revolution of 1917, anthropology in the USSR and later the Soviet Bloc countries were highly shaped by the need to conform to Marxist theories of social evolution.

British Anthropology

E.B. Tylor (1832–1917) and James George Frazer (1854–1941) are generally considered the antecedants to modern sociocultural anthropology in Britain. Though Tylor undertook a field trip to Mexico, both he and Frazer derived most of the material for their comparative studies through extensive readings of Classical materials (literature and history of Greece and Rome), the work of the early European folklorists, and reports from missionaries, travelers, and contemporaneous ethnologists. Tylor advocated strongly for unilinealism and a form of "uniformity of mankind". Tylor in particular laid the groundwork for theories of cultural diffusionism, stating that there are three ways that different groups can have similar cultural forms or technologies: "independent invention, inheritance from ancestors in a distant region, transmission from one race [sic] to another." Tylor formulated one of the early and influential anthropological conceptions of culture as "that complex whole which includes knowledge, belief, art, morals, law, custom, and any other capabilities and habits acquired by man as a member of society." However, as Stocking notes, Tylor mainly concerned himself with describing and mapping the distribution of particular elements of culture, rather than with the larger function, and generally seemed to assume a Victorian idea of progress rather than the idea of non-directional, multilineal cultural development proposed by later anthropologists. Tylor also theorized about the origins of religious feelings in human beings, proposing a theory of animism as the earliest stage, and noting that "religion" has many components, of which he believed the most important to be belief in supernatural beings (as opposed to moral systems, cosmology, etc.

James George Frazer, a Scottish scholar with a broad knowledge of Classics, also concerned himself with religion, myth, and magic. His comparative studies, most influentially in the numerous editions of The Golden Bough, analyzed similarities in religious belief and symbolism worldwide.

It is remarkable to note that neither Tylor nor Frazer, was particularly interested in fieldwork, nor were they interested in examining how the cultural elements and institutions fit together. Towards the turn of the 19th century, a number of anthropologists became dissatisfied with this categorization of cultural elements; historical reconstructions also came to seem increasingly speculative. Under the influence of several younger scholars, a new approach came to predominate among British anthropologists, concerned with analyzing how societies held together in the present (synchronic analysis, rather than diachonic or historical analysis), and emphasizing long-term (one to several years) immersion fieldwork. Cambridge University financed a multidisciplinary expedition to the Torres Strait Islands in 1898, organized by Alfred Court Haddon and including a physician-anthropologist, W. H. R. Rivers, as well as a linguist, a botanist, other specialists. The findings of the expedition set new standards for ethnographic description.

A decade and a half later, Polish-born anthropology student Brownish Malinowski (1884-1942) was beginning what he expected to be a brief period of fieldwork in the old model, collecting lists of cultural items, when the outbreak of the I World War stranded him in New Guinea. As a subject of the Austro-Hungarian Empire resident on a British colonial possession, he was effectively confined to New Guinea for several years. He made use of the time by undertaking far more intensive fieldwork than had been done by British anthropologists, and his classic ethnography, *Argonauts of the Western Pacific,* (1922) advocated an approach to fieldwork that became standard in the field: getting "the native's point of view" through participant observation. Theoretically, he advocated a functionalist interpretation, which examined how social institutions functioned to meet individual needs. And significantly British anthropology had a expansive moment in the Interwar period, with key contributors as Brownies Malinowski and Meyer Fortes.

A.R. Radcliffe-Brown also published a seminal work in 1922. He had carried out his initial fieldwork in the Andaman Islands (India) in the old style of historical reconstruction. However, after reading the work of French sociologists Émile Durkheim and Marcel Mauss, Radcliffe-Brown published an account of his research (entitled *The Andaman Islanders*) that paid close attention to the meaning and purpose of rituals and myths. Over time, he developed an approach known as structural-functionalism, which focused on how institutions in societies worked to balance out or create an equilibrium in the social system to keep it functioning harmoniously.

Further, Malinowski and Radcliffe-Brown's influence stemmed from the fact that they, like Boas, actively trained students and aggressively built up institutions that furthered their programmatic ambitions. This was particularly the case with Radcliffe-Brown, who spread his agenda for "Social Anthropology" by teaching at universities across the British Commonwealth. From the late 1930s until the postwar period appeared a string of monographs and edited volumes that cemented the paradigm of British Social Anthropology (BSA). Famous ethnographies include by Edward Evan Evans-Pritchard, and *The Dynamics of Clanship Among the Tallensi,* by Meyer Fortes; well-known edited volumes include *African Systems of Kinship and Marriage* and *African Political Systems.*

Notably Max Gluckman, together with many of his colleagues at the Rhodes-Livingstone Institute and students at Manchester University, collectively known as the Manchester School, took BSA in new directions through their introduction of explicitly Marxist-informed theory, their emphasis on conflicts and conflict resolution, and their attention to the ways in which individuals negotiate and make use of the social structural possibilities. Later in the 1960s and 1970s, Edmund Leach and his students Mary Douglas and Nur Yalman, among others, introduced French structuralism in the style of Lévi-Strauss; while British anthropology has continued to emphasize social organization and economics over purely symbolic or literary topics, differences among British, French, and American sociocultural anthropologies have diminished with increasing dialogue and borrowing of both theory and methods.

Today, social anthropology in Britain engages internationally with many other social theories and has branched in many directions. In countries of the British Commonwealth, social anthropology has often been institutionally separate from physical anthropology and primatology, which may be connected with departments of biology or zoology; and from archaeology, which may be connected with departments of Classics, Egyptology, and the like. In other countries (and in some, particularly smaller, British and North American universities), anthropologists have also found themselves institutionally linked with scholars of folklore, museum studies, human geography, sociology, social relations, ethnic studies, cultural studies, and social work.

US Anthropology

From its beginnings in the early 19th century through the early 20th century, anthropology in the United States was influenced by the presence of Native American societies. As in other colonial powers (including Britain, France, Spain, Portugal, and the countries of Latin America) this encounter with colonial subjects manifested in several ways. Curiosity, admiration, desire to "reform" or "civilize" native practices, or simple puzzlement at how societies could function with such different social and political systems, all motivated early ethnographers. Practical concerns of Christian missionaries and colonial administrators, seeking to communicate with native peoples or figure out how to incorporate them, helped gain funding and institutional attention. Statements of ethnologists (as well as many amateurs, missionaries, and colonial administrators, who were not clearly distinguished from more committed scholars in this era prior to professionalization of anthropology) often played into political debates around the definition humanity and citizenship.

These conflicts between what may be seen as the pursuit of pure knowledge or the facilitation of intercultural understanding on the one hand, and the potentially exploitative, oppressive, or coercive uses to which that knowledge might be put, on the other, concerned many early anthropologists and has become a major source of controversy and self-examination within the discipline since at least the mid-20th century. The claim that anthropology accompliced to the "project of colonialism" is a misconception mostly based on few "slander pieces" from the 1960s and seventies.

Cultural anthropology in the United States was influenced greatly by the ready availability of Native American societies as ethnographic subjects. The field was pioneered by staff of the Bureau of Indian Affairs and the Smithsonian Institution's Bureau of American Ethnology, men such as

John Wesley Powell and Frank Hamilton Cushing. Lewis Henry Morgan (1818-1881), a lawyer from Rochester, New York, became an advocate for and ethnological scholar of the Iroquois. His comparative analyses of religion, government, material culture, and especially kinship patterns proved to be influential contributions to the field of anthropology. Like other scholars of his day , Morgan argued that human societies could be classified into categories of cultural evolution on a scale of progression that ranged from *savagery*, to *barbarism*, to *civilization*. Generally, Morgan used technology (such as bowmaking or pottery) as an indicator of position on this scale.

Franz Boas established academic anthropology in the United States in opposition to this sort of evolutionary perspective. Boasian anthropology was politically active and suspicious of research dictated by the U.S. government and wealthy patrons. It was rigorously empirical and skeptical of overgeneralizations and attempts to establish universal laws. Boas studied immigrant children to demonstrate that biological race was not immutable, and that human conduct and behavior resulted from nurture, rather than nature.

Under the influence of the German tradition, Boas argued that the world was full of distinct *cultures,* rather than societies whose evolution could be measured by how much or how little "civilization" they had. He was of the opinion believed that each culture has to be studied in its particularity, and argued that cross-cultural generalizations, like those made in the natural sciences, were not possible. In doing so, he fought discrimination against immigrants, African Americans, and Native North Americans. Many American anthropologists adopted his agenda for social reform, and theories of race continue to be popular targets for anthropologists today. The so-called "Four Field Approach" has its origins in Boasian Anthropology, dividing the discipline in the four crucial and interrelated fields of sociocultural, biological, linguistic, and prehistoric anthropology.

Boas used his positions at Columbia University and the American Museum of Natural History to train and develop multiple generations of students. His first generation of students included Alfred Kroeber, Robert Lowie, Edward Sapir and Ruth Benedict, all of whom produced richly detailed studies of indigenous North American cultures. They provided a wealth of details used to attack the theory of a single evolutionary process. Kroeber and Sapir's focus on Native American languages helped establish linguistics as a truly general science and free it from its historical focus on Indo-European languages.

Remarkably, the publication of Alfred Kroeber's textbook, *Anthropology,* marked a turning point in American anthropology. After three decades of amassing material, Boasians felt a growing urge to generalize. This was most obvious in the 'Culture and Personality' studies carried out by younger Boasians such as Margaret Mead and Ruth Benedict. Influenced by psychoanalytic psychologists such as Sigmund Freud and Carl Jung, these authors sought to understand the way that individual personalities were shaped by the wider cultural and social forces in which they grew up. Though such works as *Coming of Age in Samoa* and *The Chrysanthemum and the Sword* remain popular with the American public, Mead and Benedict never had the impact on the discipline of anthropology that some expected.

Canadian Anthropology

Canadian anthropology in began, as in other parts of the Colonial world, as ethnological data in the records of travellers and missionaries. In Canada, Jesuit missionaries such as Fathers LeClercq, Le Jeune and Sagard, in the 1600s, provide the oldest ethnographic records of native tribes in what was then the Domain of Canada.

True anthropology began with a Government department: the Geological Survey of Canada, and George Mercer Dawson (director in 1895). Dawson's support for anthropology created impetus for the profession in Canada. This was expanded upon by Prime Minister Wilfrid Laurier, who established a Division of Anthropology within the Geological Survey in 1910. Anthropologists were recruited from England and the USA, setting the foundation for the unique Canadian style of anthropology. Early scholars include the brilliant linguist and Boasian, Edward Sapir, also Oxford graduates Marius Barbeau and Diamond Jenness. Born in rural Québec, Barbeau became a Rhodes scholar and eventually a classmate of Jenness. The two studied under Tylor and Marett at Oxford. In Canada, Barbeau and Jenness worked at the National Museum (as it became known later). In 1944, Canada's first home-grown anthropologist established the archive which has become a key source of ethnographic and folklore material.

Following George Mercer Dawson (of McGill, Montreal) and Franz Boas, Sapir and Barbeau conducted ethnographic research and collected material culture from the peoples of the Northwest Coast, especially Haida. Jenness is best known for his research in the Arctic among the Copper Inuit. However, in actuality, they all worked in a variety of areas in Canada, recording traditions and songs, studying languages, and collecting artifacts for the museum. They essentially had sole responsibility for the development of the profession in Canada from 1910 until 1925 when Sapir left. The development was slow relative to expansion (due to the colonizing needs) of Britain and the USA.

Now Anthropology in academics, the first academic position in anthropology at a Canadian university was awarded to Thomas McIlwraith at the University of Toronto in 1925. The next universities to hire anthropologists, UBC and McGill, did so only in 1947. The first PhD in anthropology was granted in 1956, with only a few more being granted until the late 1960s. The 1970s brought a boom in university development and in professional anthropology, and by 1980 about 400 people with doctorates in anthropology were employed in Canada, and many more with a master's degree. Harry Hawthorne built the department at UBC and set a standard for the use of anthropological research as a guide to public policy in his classic report to the federal government, coauthored by M.-A. Tremblay, "A Survey of the Contemporary Indians of Canada" (1966, 1967). Canadian Anthropology is characterized by a combination of Americanist Boasian-influenced interest in Native American tribes and peoples, British Anthropological concerns with social function and process, and Francophone concerns with small, rural and ethnically isolated community studies. Issues of disparity, continuity and change, political-economy, environment and cultural ecology, and personality, culture and symbolism predominated the discourse from World War I to the Vietnam War era.

French Anthropology

After Great Britain in Europe, Anthropology in France has a less clear genealogy than the British and American traditions, in part because many French writers influential in anthropology have been trained or held faculty positions in sociology, philosophy, or other fields rather than in anthropology. Most commentators consider Marcel Mauss (1872-1950), nephew of the renowned sociologist Émile Durkheim to be the founder of the French anthropological tradition. Mauss belonged to Durkheim's Année Sociologique group; and while Durkheim and others examined the state of modern societies, Mauss and his collaborators (such as Henri Hubert and Robert Hertz) drew on ethnography and philology to analyze societies which were not as 'differentiated' as European nation states. Two works by Mauss in particular proved to have enduring relevance: *Essay on the Gift* a seminal analysis of exchange and reciprocity, and his Huxley lecture on the notion of the person, the first comparative study of notions of person and selfhood cross-culturally. Unlike in English, in French there's no clear differentiation among ethnology, social anthropology and cultural anthropology.

Throughout the interwar years, French interest in anthropology often dovetailed with wider cultural movements such as surrealism and primitivism which drew on ethnography for inspiration. Marcel Griaule and Michel Leiris are examples of people who combined anthropology with the French avant-garde. During this time most of what is known as *ethnologie* was restricted to museums, such as the Musée de l'Homme founded by Paul Rivet, and anthropology had a close relationship with studies of folklore.

However, it was Claude Lévi-Strauss who helped institutionalize anthropology in France. In addition to the enormous influence his structuralism exerted across multiple disciplines, Lévi-Strauss established ties with American and British anthropologists. At the same time he established centers and laboratories within France to provide an institutional context within anthropology while training influential students such as Maurice Godelier and Françoise Héritier who would prove influential in the world of French anthropology. Much of the distinct character of France's anthropology today is a result of the fact that most anthropology is carried out in nationally funded research laboratories (CNRS) rather than academic departments in universities.

Other influential writers in the 1970s include Pierre Clastres, who explains in his books on the Guayaki tribe in Paraguay that "primitive societies" actively oppose the institution of the state. Therefore, these stateless societies are not less evolved than societies with states, but took the active choice of conjuring the institution of authority as a separate function from society. The leader is only a spokesperson for the group when it has to deal with other groups ("international relations") but has no inside authority, and may be violently removed if he attempts to abuse this position.

The most important French social theorist since Foucault and Lévi-Strauss is Pierre Bourdieu, who trained formally in philosophy and sociology and eventually held the Chair of Sociology at the Collège de France. Like Mauss and others before him, however, he worked on topics both in sociology and anthropology. His fieldwork among the Kabyles of Algeria places him solidly in anthropology, while his analysis of the function and reproduction of fashion and cultural capital in European societies places him as solidly in sociology.

Other Countries

Anthropology in Greece and Portugal is much influenced by British anthropology. In Greece, there was since the

19th century a science of the folklore called *laographia* (laography), in the form of "a science of the interior", although theoretically weak; but the connotation of the field deeply changed after World War II, when a wave of Anglo-American anthropologists introduced a science "of the outside". In Italy, the development of ethnology and related studies did not received as much attention as other branches of learning.

Germany and Norway are the countries that showed the most division and conflict between scholars focusing on domestic socio-cultural issues and scholars focusing on "other" societies.

Anglophone Anthropology

Before World War II British 'social anthropology' and American 'cultural anthropology' were still distinct traditions. After the war, enough British and American anthropologists either borrowed ideas and approaches from each other that some began to speak of them collectively as 'sociocultural' anthropology.

During 1950s and mid-1960s anthropology tended increasingly to model itself after the natural sciences. Some anthropologists, such as Lloyd Fallers and Clifford Geertz, focused on processes of modernization by which newly independent states could develop. Others, such as Julian Steward and Leslie White, focused on how societies evolve and fit their ecological niche — an approach popularized by Marvin Harris. Economic anthropology as influenced by Karl Polanyi and practiced by Marshall Sahlins and George Dalton focused on how traditional economics ignored cultural and social factors. In England, British Social Anthropology's paradigm began to fragment as Max Gluckman and Peter Worsley experimented with Marxism and authors such as Rodney Needham and Edmund Leach incorporated Lévi-Strauss's structuralism into their work.

Structuralism also influenced a number of developments in 1960s and 1970s, including cognitive anthropology and componential analysis. Authors such as David Schneider, Clifford Geertz, and Marshall Sahlins developed a more fleshed-out concept of culture as a web of meaning or signification, which proved very popular within and beyond the discipline. In keeping with the times, much of anthropology became politicized through the Algerian War of Independence and opposition to the Vietnam War; Marxism became a more and more popular theoretical approach in the discipline. By the 1970s the authors of volumes such as *Reinventing Anthropology* worried about anthropology's relevance.

In the 1980s issues of power, such as those examined in Eric Wolf's *Europe and the People Without History*, were central to the discipline. Books like *Anthropology and the Colonial Encounter* pondered anthropology's ties to colonial inequality, while the immense popularity of theorists such as Antonio Gramsci and Michel Foucault moved issues of power and hegemony into the spotlight. Gender and sexuality became popular topics, as did the relationship between history and anthropology, influenced by Marshall Sahlins (again), who drew on Lévi-Strauss and Fernand Braudel to examine the relationship between social structure and individual agency. Also influential in these issues were Nietzsche, Heidegger, the critical theory of the Frankfurt School, Derrida and Lacan.

In the late 1980s and 1990s authors such as George Marcus and James Clifford pondered ethnographic authority, particularly how and why anthropological knowledge was possible and authoritative. They were reflecting trends in research and discourse initiated by Feminists in the academy, although they excused themselves from commenting specifically on those pioneering critics. Nevertheless, key aspects of feminist theorsing and methods became de rigeur as part of the 'post-modern moment' in anthropology: Ethnographies became more reflexive, explicitly addressing the author's methodology, cultural, gender and racial positioning, and their influence on his or her ethnographic analysis. This was part of a more general trend of postmodernism that was popular contemporaneously. Currently anthropologists have begun to pay attention to globalization, medicine and biotechnology, indigenous rights, and the anthropology of industrialized societies.

Approaches to Anthropology

The "four field" approach

Principally in the United States, anthropology is often defined as being "holistic" and based on a "four-field" approach. There is an ongoing dispute on this view; supporters consider anthropology holistic in two senses: it is concerned with all human beings across times and places, and with all dimensions of humanity (evolutionary, biophysical, sociopolitical, economic, cultural, psychological, etc.); also many academic programs following this approach take a "four-field" approach to anthropology that encompasses physical anthropology, archeology, linguistics, and cultural anthropology or social anthropology. The definition of anthropology as holistic and the "four-field" approach are disputed by some leading anthropologists, that consider those as artifacts from 19th century social evolutionary thought that inappropriately impose scientific positivism upon cultural anthropology. While originating in the US, both the four field approach and debates concerning it have been exported internationally under American academic influence.

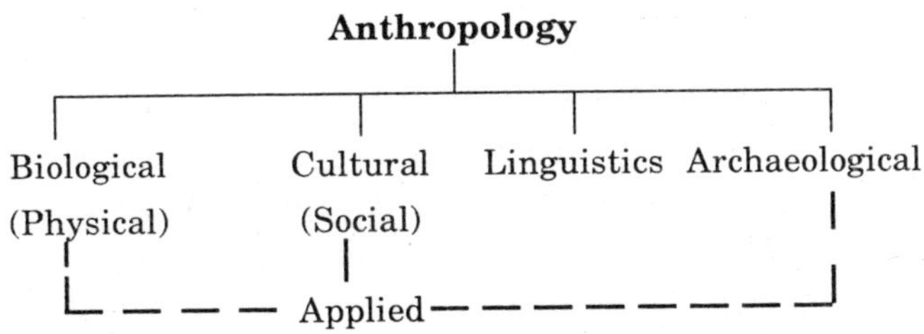

Main Branches of Anthropology

The four fields are:

- *Biological or physical anthropology* seeks to understand the physical human being through the study of human evolution and adaptability, population genetics, and primatology. Subfields or related fields include anthropometrics, forensic anthropology, osteology, and nutritional anthropology.
- *Socio-cultural anthropology* is the investigation, often through long term, intensive field studies (including participant-observation methods), of the culture and social organization of a particular people: language, economic and political organization, law and conflict resolution, patterns of consumption and exchange, kinship and family structure, gender relations, childrearing and socialization, religion, mythology, symbolism, etc. (U.S. universities more often use the term cultural anthropology; British universities have tended to call the corresponding field social anthropology, and for much of the 20th century emphasized

the analysis of social organization more than cultural symbolism.) In some European countries, socio-cultural anthropology is known as ethnology (a term also used in English-speaking countries to denote the comparative aspect of socio-cultural anthropology.) Subfields and related fields include psychological anthropology, folklore, anthropology of religion, ethnic studies, cultural studies, anthropology of media and cyberspace, and study of the diffusion of social practices and cultural forms.

- *Linguistic anthropology* seeks to understand the processes of human communications, verbal and non-verbal, variation in language across time and space, the social uses of language, and the relationship between language and culture. It identifies the many subtle elements of the world's languages, and documents their structure, function and history. Subfields include anthropological linguistics. Linguistic anthropologists often draw on related fields including sociolinguistics, cognitive linguistics, semiotics, discourse analysis, and narrative analysis.
- *Archaeology* studies the contemporary distribution and form of artifacts (materials modified by past human activities), with the intent of understanding distribution and movement of ancient populations, development of human social organization, and relationships among contemporary populations; it also contributes significantly to the work of population geneticists, historical linguists, and many historians.

> Archaeology involves a wide variety of field techniques (remote sensing, survey, geophysical studies, coring, excavation) and laboratory procedures (compositional analyses, dating studies (radiocarbon, optically stimulated luminescence dating), measures of formal variability, examination of wear patterns, residue analyses, etc.). Archaeologists predominantly study materials produced by prehistoric groups but also includes modern, historical and ethnographic populations. Archaeology is usually regarded as a separate (but related) field outside North America, although closely related to the anthropological field of material culture, which deals with physical objects created or used within a living or past group as a means of understanding its cultural values.

A number of subfield or modes of anthropology cut across these divisions. For example, medical anthropology is often considered a subfield of socio-cultural anthropology; however, many anthropologists who study medical topics also look at biological variation in populations or the interaction of culture and biology. They may also use linguistic analysis to understand communication around health and illness, or archaeological techniques to understand health and illness in historical or prehistorical populations. Similarly, forensic anthropologists may use both techniques from both physical anthropology and archaeology, and may also practice as medical anthropologists. Biocultural anthropology is a broad term used to describe syntheses of cultural and biological perspectives. Applied anthropology is perhaps better considered an emphasis than a subfield in the same sense as the standard four; applied anthropologists may work for government agencies, nongovernmental agencies, or private industry, using techniques from any of the subfields to address matters such as policy implementation, impact assessments, education, marketing research, or product development.

More recently, anthropology programs at several prominent U.S. universities have begun dividing the field into two: one emphasizing the humanities, critical theory, and interpretive or semotic approaches; the other emphasizing evolutionary theory, quantitive methods, and explicit theory testing (over idiographic description), though there have also been institutional pressures to rejoin at least one high-profile split department. At some universitities, biological anthropology and archaelogy programs have also moved from departments of anthropology to departments of biology or other related fields. This has occasioned much discussion within the American Anthropological Association, and it remains to be seen whether some form of the four-field organization will persist in North American universities.

As might be inferred from the above list of subfields, anthropology is a methodologically diverse discipline, incorporating both qualitative methods and quantitative methods. Ethnographies—intensive case studies based on field research—have historically had a central place in the literature of sociocultural and linguistic anthropology, but are increasingly supplemented by mixed-methods approaches. Currently, technological advancements are spurring methodological innovation across anthropology's subfields. Radiocarbon dating, population genetics, GPS, and digitial video- and audio-recording are just a few of the many technologies spurring new developments in anthropological research.

Recent Developments

It is significant to note that during the first four decades of the 20th century, American cultural anthropology developed under the powerful influence of Franz Boas and his students and their struggle against racial determinism and the ethnocentrism of 19th-century cultural evolutionism. With the additional impact of the Great Depression and World War II, American anthropology developed a pronounced liberal-left tone by the 1950s. However, the discipline's deep involvement with nonwestern cultures put it in a vulnerable position during the campus upheavals of the late 1960s and in the subsequent "culture wars." The "politics of anthropology" has become a pervasive concern since then. Whatever the realities, the notion of anthropology as somehow complicit in morally unacceptable projects has become a significant topic both within the discipline and in "cultural studies" and "post-colonialism," etc.

A few of the central elements in this discourse are the following:

- The claim that the discipline grew out of colonialism, perhaps was in league with it, and derived some of its key notions from it, consciously or not. It is often assumed that an example of this exploitative relationship can be seen in the relationship between British anthropologists and colonial forces in Africa, yet this assumption has not been supported by much evidence.
- The idea that social and political problems must arise because anthropologists usually have more power than the people they study; it is a form of colonialist theft in which the anthropologist gains power at the expense of subjects (Rabinow, Dwyer, McGrane). Anthropologists, they argue, can gain

yet more power by exploiting knowledge and artifacts of the people they study while the people they study gain nothing, or even lose, in the exchange. Little critical writing has been published in response to these wide-ranging claims, themselves the product of the political concerns and atmosphere of their own times.

- It is claimed the discipline was ahistorical, and dealt with its "objects" (sic) "out of time," to their detriment (Fabian). It is often claimed that anthropologists regularly "exoticized 'the Other,'" or, with equal assurance, that they inappropriately universalized "Others" and "human nature." However this misconception on the nature of anthropology is falsified by the existence many works focusing on peoples and topics very close to the author's "home".
- Other more explicitly political concerns have to do with anthropologists' entanglements with government intelligence agencies, on the one hand, and anti-war politics on the other. Franz Boas publicly objected to US participation in World War I, and after the war he published a brief expose and condemnation of the participation of several American archeologists in espionage in Mexico under their cover as scientists. But by the 1940s, many of Boas' anthropologist contemporaries were active in the allied war effort against the "Axis" (Nazi Germany, Fascist Italy, and Imperial Japan). Many served in the armed forces but others worked in intelligence (for example, Office of Strategic Services (OSS) and the Office of War Information). David H.

> Price's work on American anthropology during the Cold War provides detailed accounts of the pursuit and dismissal of several anthropologists for their vocal left-wing sympathies. On the other hand, attempts to accuse anthropologists of complicity with the CIA and government intelligence activities during the Vietnam War years have turned up surprisingly little.

On the contrary, many anthropologists (students and teachers) were active in the antiwar movement and a great many resolutions condemning the war in all its aspects were passed overwhelmingly at the annual meetings of the American Anthropological Association (AAA). In the decades since the Vietnam war the tone of cultural and social anthropology, at least, has been increasingly politicized, with the dominant liberal tone of earlier generations replaced with one more radical, a mix of, and varying degrees of, Marxist, feminist, anarchist, post-colonial, post-modern, Saidian, Foucauldian, identity-based, and more.

Professional anthropological bodies often object to the use of anthropology for the benefit of the state. Their codes of ethics or statements may proscribe anthropologists from giving secret briefings. The Association of Social Anthropologists of the UK and Commonwealth (ASA) has called certain scholarships ethically dangerous. The AAA's current 'Statement of Professional Responsibility' clearly states that "in relation with their own government and with host governments... no secret research, no secret reports or debriefings of any kind should be agreed to or given."

More recently, there have been concerns expressed about bioprospecting, along with struggles for self-representation for native peoples and the repatriation of indigenous remains and material culture, with anthropologists often in the lead on these issues.

Other political controversies come from the emphasis in American anthropology on cultural relativism and its long-standing dismissal of the concept of race. The development of sociobiology in the late 1960s was opposed by cultural anthropologists such as Marshall Sahlins, who argued that these positions were reductive. While authors such John Randal Baker continued to develop the biological concept of race into the 1970s, the rise of genetics has proven to be central to developments on this front. As genetics continues to advance as a science, scholars such as Luca Cavalli-Sforza have continued to transform and advance notions of race through the use of recent developments in genetics, such as tracing past migrations of peoples through their mitochondrial and Y-chromosomal DNA, and ancestry-informative markers.

It is often argued that Anthropology originated and developed as the study of the "Other", both in terms of time (past societies) and space (non-European/non-Western societies). However there exist many works focusing on peoples and topics very close to the author's "home". It is also argued that other fields of study, like History and Sociology, on the contrary focus disproportionately on the West.

In France, the study of existing contemporary society has been traditionally left to sociologists, but this is increasingly changing, starting in the 1970s from scholars like Isac Chiva and journals like *Terrain* ("fieldwork"), and developing with the center founded by Marc Augé (*Le Centre d'anthropologie des mondes contemporains*, the Anthropological Research Center of Contemporary Societies).

The same approach of focusing on "modern world" topics by *Terrain*, was also present in the British Manchester School of the 1950s.

It has been reported that there has been an "institutional and academic apartheid" between the two sorts of anthropology, the one focusing on the "Other" and the one focusing on the "Self" contemporary society; an apartheid ranging from a "no contact" status to even open conflict. The countries where this was greater were Germany and Norway, but it was also significant in the 1980s France.

The relations with the natural sciences and the Humanities

The pressure for the "integration" of socio-cultural anthropology (inherently associated with the humanities), with "biological-physical anthropology" (inherently associated with the natural sciences), has been criticized as an inappropriate imposition of positivism (the belief that the only proper knowledge is that derived from the scientific method) upon cultural anthropology. This criticism argument has been raised towards the development of sociobiology in the late 1960s (by cultural anthropologists such as Marshall Sahlins), and towards the "four field holism" of American Anthropology.

Applied Anthropology

Basically Applied anthropology refers to the application of method and theory in anthropology to the analysis and solution of practical problems. Inasmuch as anthropology proper comprises four main subdisciplines — biological, cultural, linguistic, and archeological anthropology — the practical application of any of these subdisciplines may properly be designated "applied anthropology. Indeed, some practical problems may invoke all subdisciplines. For example, a Native American community development program may involve archeological research to determine legitimacy of water rights claims, ethnography may involve assessing the current and recent historical cultural characteristics of the community, linguistics may be applied to restoring language competetence, and biological, or more specifically "medical" anthropology may be applied to determine the factors contributing to dietary deficiency diseases, etc.

Pertiently some regard applied anthropology to be a fifth subdiscipline of anthropology that applies anthropological data, perspectives, theory, and methods to identify, assess and solve contemporary social problems.

Applied anthropologists often work for nonacademic clients such as governments, development agencies, nongovernmental organizations (NGOs), tribal and ethnic associations, interest groups, social-service and educational agencies, and businesses. Ethnography and participant observation are the applied anthropologist's primary research tools. They also use textual analysis, survey research and other empirical methods to inform policy or to market products. An applied anthropologist is often likely to be employed in a non-academic setting.

This is a contrast to more academic sociocultural anthropology, which may be more concerned with creating theoretical models which correspond to its units of analysis, e.g. social inequality, performance, exchange, meaning, and so forth. Sometimes the research that falls within the applied field is referred to as "applied" in contrast to academic research, which is referred to as "basic." Business anthropology is an example of "applied" anthropology.

Examples of questions that an applied anthropologist would attempt to solve might be:

- How can public health authorities promote condom use amongst members of a particular subculture?
- Why do people migrate to XYZ place or from ABC place?

The premiere journal in the US of applied anthropology is Human Organization published by the Society for Applied Anthropology.

Under the directorship of the RAI, Jonathan Benthall, author of *The Best of Anthropology Today*, created the annual The Lucy Mair Medal of Applied Anthropology. This recognizes excellence in using anthropology "for the relief of poverty or distress, or for the active recognition of human dignity."

The foregoing discussion has made it clear that what is the discipline of Anthropology. We have come to know about the development and growth of the discipline from different angles.

2

EVOLUTION OF HUMAN BEING

Human evolution (which is the major theme of the discipline of Anthropology) is the part of biological evolution concerning the emergence of humans as a distinct species. It is the subject of a broad scientific inquiry that seeks to understand and describe how this change and development occurred. The study of human evolution encompasses many scientific disciplines, most notably physical anthropology, linguistics and genetics. The term "human", in the context of human evolution, refers to the genus *Homo*, but studies of human evolution usually include other hominins, such as the australopithecines.

Paleoanthropology

Paleoanthropology is the study of ancient humans based on fossil evidence, tools, and other signs of human habitation. The modern field of paleoanthropology began in the 19th century with the discovery of "Neanderthal man". The eponymous skeleton was found in 1856, but there had been finds elsewhere since 1830. By 1859, the morphological similarity of humans to certain great apes had been discussed and argued for some time, but the idea of the biological evolution of species in general was not legitimized until Charles Darwin published *On the Origin of Species* in November of that year. Darwin's first book on evolution did not address the specific question of human evolution: "Light will be thrown on the origin of man and his history," was all Darwin wrote on the subject. Nevertheless, the implications of evolutionary theory were clear to contemporary readers.

Debates between Thomas Huxley and Richard Owen focused on human evolution. Huxley convincingly illustrated many of the similarities and differences between humans and apes in his 1863 book *Evidence as to Man's Place in Nature*. By the time Darwin published his own book on the subject, *The Descent of Man*, it was already a well-known interpretation of his theory, and the interpretation which made the theory highly controversial. Even many of Darwin's original supporters (such as Alfred Russel Wallace and Charles Lyell) balked at the idea that human beings could have evolved their impressive mental capacities and moral sensibilities through natural selection.

Since the time of Carolus Linnaeus, scientists have considered the great apes to be the closest relatives of human beings, based on morphological similarity. In the 19th century, they speculated that the closest living relatives of humans are chimpanzees and gorillas. Based on the natural range of these creatures, they surmised that humans share a common ancestor with other African apes and that fossils of these ancestors would ultimately be found in Africa.

It was not until the 1920s that hominid fossils were discovered in Africa. In 1924, Raymond Dart described *Australopithecus africanus*. The type specimen was the Taung Child, an australopithecine infant discovered in a cave deposit being mined for concrete at Taung, South Africa. The remains were a remarkably well-preserved tiny skull and an endocranial cast of the individual's brain. Although the brain was small (410 cm^3), its shape was rounded, unlike that of chimpanzees and gorillas, and more like a modern human brain. Also, the specimen exhibited short canine teeth, and the position of the foramen magnum was evidence of bipedal locomotion. All of these traits convinced Dart that the Taung baby was a bipedal human ancestor, a transitional form between apes and humans.

Another 20 years would pass before Dart's claims were taken seriously, following the discovery of more fossils that resembled his find. The prevailing view of the time was that a large brain evolved before bipedality. It was thought that intelligence on par with modern humans was a prerequisite to bipedalism.

The australopithecines are now thought to be immediate ancestors of the genus *Homo*, the group to which modern humans belong. Both australopithecines and *Homo sapiens* are part of the tribe Hominini, but recent data has brought into doubt the position of *A. africanus* as a direct ancestor of modern humans; it may well have been a dead-end cousin. The australopithecines were originally classified as either gracile or robust. The robust variety of *Australopithecus* has since been reclassified as *Paranthropus*, although it is still regarded as a subgenus of *Australopithecus* by some authors.

In the 1930s, when the robust specimens were first described, the *Paranthropus* genus was used. During the 1960s, the robust variety was moved into *Australopithecus*. The recent trend has been back to the original classification as a separate genus.

Before *Homo*

The evolutionary history of the primates can be traced back for some 85 million years, as one of the oldest of all surviving placental mammal groups. Most paleontologists consider that primates share a common ancestor with the bats, another extremely ancient lineage, and that this ancestor probably lived during the late Cretaceous together with the last dinosaurs. The oldest known primates come from North America, but they were widespread in Eurasia and Africa as well, during the tropical conditions of the Paleocene and Eocene.

With the beginning of modern climates, marked by the formation of the first Antarctic ice in the early Oligocene around 40 million years ago, primates went extinct everywhere but Africa and southern Asia. Fossil evidence found in Germany 20 years ago was determined to be about 16.5 million years old, some 1.5 million years older than similar species from East Africa. It suggests that the great ape and human lineage first appeared in Eurasia and not in Africa.

The discoveries suggest that the early ancestors of the hominids (the family of great apes and humans) migrated to Eurasia from Africa about 17 million years ago, just before these two continents were cut off from each other by an expansion of the Mediterranean Sea. Begun says that the great apes flourished in Eurasia and that their lineage leading to the African apes and humans—Dryopithecus—migrated south from Europe or Western Asia into Africa. The surviving tropical population, which is seen most completely in the upper Eocene and lowermost Oligocene fossil beds of the Fayum depression southwest of Cairo, gave rise to all living primates—lemurs of Madagascar, lorises of Southeast Asia, galagos or "bush babies" of Africa, and the anthropoids; platyrrhines or New World monkeys, and catarrhines or Old World monkeys and the great apes and humans.

The earliest known catarrhine is *Kamoyapithecus* from uppermost Oligocene at Eragaleit in the northern Kenya rift valley, dated to 24 Ma (millions of years before present). Its ancestry is generally thought to be close to such genera as *Aegyptopithecus*, *Propliopithecus*, and *Parapithecus* from the Fayum, at around 35 mya. There are no fossils from the intervening 11 million years. No near ancestor to South American platyrrhines, whose fossil record begins at around 30 mya, can be identified among the North African fossil species, and possibly lies in other forms that lived in West Africa that were caught up in the still-mysterious transatlantic sweepstakes that sent primates, rodents, boa constrictors, and cichlid fishes from Africa to South America sometime in the Oligocene.

In the early Miocene, after 22 mya, many kinds of arboreally adapted primitive catarrhines from East Africa suggest a long history of prior diversification. Because the fossils at 20 mya include fragments attributed to *Victoriapithecus*, the earliest cercopithecoid, the other forms are (by default) grouped as hominoids, without clear evidence as to which are closest to living apes and humans. Among the presently recognized genera in this group, which ranges up to 13 mya, we find *Proconsul*, *Rangwapithecus*, *Dendropithecus*, *Limnopithecus*, *Nacholapithecus*, *Equatorius*, *Nyanzapithecus*, *Afropithecus*, *Heliopithecus*, and *Kenyapithecus*, all from East Africa. The presence of other generalized non-cercopithecids of middle Miocene age from sites far distant—*Otavipithecus* from cave deposits in Namibia, and *Pierolapithecus* and *Dryopithecus* from

France, Spain and Austria—is evidence of a wide diversity of forms across Africa and the Mediterranean basin during the relatively warm and equable climatic regimes of the early and middle Miocene. The youngest of the Miocene hominoids, *Oreopithecus*, is from 9 mya coal beds in Italy.

Molecular evidence indicates that the lineage of gibbons (family Hylobatidae) became distinct between 18 and 12 Ma, and that of orangutans (subfamily Ponginae) at about 12 Ma; we have no fossils that clearly document the ancestry of gibbons, which may have originated in a so far unknown South East Asian hominid population, but fossil proto-orangutans may be represented by *Ramapithecus* from India and *Griphopithecus* from Turkey, dated to around 10 Ma.

Molecular evidence further suggests that between 8 and 4 mya, first the gorillas, and then the chimpanzee (genus *Pan*) split off from the line leading to the humans; human DNA is 98.4 percent identical to the DNA of chimpanzees. We have no fossil record, however, of either group of African great apes, possibly because bones do not fossilize in rain forest environments.

Hominines, however, seem to have been one of the mammal groups (as well as antelopes, hyenas, dogs, pigs, elephants, and horses) that adapted to the open grasslands as soon as this biome appeared, due to increasingly seasonal climates, about 8 mya, and their fossils are relatively well known. The earliest are *Sahelanthropus tchadensis* (7–6 mya) and *Orrorin tugenensis* (6 mya), followed by:

- *Ardipithecus* (5.5–4.4 mya), with species *Ar. kadabba* and *Ar. ramidus*;
- *Australopithecus* (4–2 mya), with species *Au.*

anamensis, *Au. afarensis*, *Au. africanus*, *Au. bahrelghazali*, and *Au. garhi*;
- *Paranthropus* (3–1.2 mya), with species *P. aethiopicus*, *P. boisei*, and *P. robustus*;
- *Homo* (2 mya–present).

The Genus *Homo*

The word *homo* is Latin for "human", chosen originally by Carolus Linnaeus in his classification system. It is often translated as "man", although this can lead to confusion, given that the English word "man" can be generic like *homo*, but can also specifically refer to males. Latin for "man" in the gender-specific sense is *vir*, cognate with "*vir*ile" and "*were*wolf". The word "human" is from *humanus*, the adjectival form of *homo*.

In modern taxonomy, *Homo sapiens* is the only extant species of its genus, *Homo*. Likewise, the ongoing study of the origins of *Homo sapiens* often demonstrates that there were other *Homo* species, all of which are now extinct. While some of these other species might have been ancestors of *H. sapiens*, many were likely our "cousins", having speciated away from our ancestral line. There is not yet a consensus as to which of these groups should count as separate species and which as subspecies of another species. In some cases this is due to the paucity of fossils, in other cases it is due to the slight differences used to classify species in the *Homo* genus. The Sahara pump theory provides an explanation of the early variation in the genus *Homo*.

Homo Habilis

H. habilis lived from about 2.4 to 1.5 million years ago (mya). *H. habilis*, the first species of the genus *Homo*, evolved in South and East Africa in the late Pliocene or early Pleistocene, 2.5–2 mya, when it diverged from the

Australopithecines. *H. habilis* had smaller molars and larger brains than the Australopithecines, and made tools from stone and perhaps animal bones. One of the first known hominids, it was nicknamed 'handy man' by its discoverer, Louis Leakey. Some scientists have proposed moving this species out of *Homo* and into *Australopithecus*.

Homo Rudolfensis *and* Homo Georgicus

These are proposed species names for fossils from about 1.9–1.6 mya, the relation of which with *H. habilis* is not yet clear.

- *H. rudolfensis* refers to a single, incomplete skull from Kenya.
- *H. georgicus*, from Georgia, may be an intermediate form between *H. habilis* and *H. erectus*, or a sub-species of *H. erectus*.

Homo ergaster and Homo erectus

The first fossils of *Homo erectus* were discovered by Dutch physician Eugene Dubois in 1891 on the Indonesian island of Java. He originally gave the material the name *Pithecanthropus erectus* based on its morphology that he considered to be intermediate between that of humans and apes. *H. erectus* lived from about 1.8 mya to 70,000 years ago. Often the early phase, from 1.8 to 1.25 mya, is considered to be a separate species, *H. ergaster*, or it is seen as a subspecies of erectus, *Homo erectus ergaster*.

In the Early Pleistocene, 1.5–1 mya, in Africa, Asia, and Europe, presumably, *Homo habilis* evolved larger brains and made more elaborate stone tools; these differences and others are sufficient for anthropologists to classify them as a new species, *H. erectus*. In addition *H. erectus* was the first human ancestor to walk truly upright. This was made possible by the evolution of locking knees and a different location of the foramen magnum (the hole in the skull where the spine enters). They may have used fire to cook their meat.

A famous example of *Homo erectus* is Peking Man; others were found in Asia (notably in Indonesia), Africa, and Europe. Many paleoanthropologists are now using the term *Homo ergaster* for the non-Asian forms of this group, and reserving *H. erectus* only for those fossils found in the Asian region and meeting certain skeletal and dental requirements which differ slightly from ergaster.

Homo cepranensis and Homo antecessor

These are proposed as species that may be intermediate between *H. erectus* and *H. heidelbergensis*.

- *H. cepranensis* refers to a single skull cap from Italy, estimated to be about 800,000 years old.
- *H. antecessor* is known from fossils from Spain and England that are 800,000–500,000 years old.

Homo heidelbergensis

H. heidelbergensis (Heidelberg Man) lived from about 800,000 to about 300,000 years ago. Also proposed as *Homo sapiens heidelbergensis* or *Homo sapiens paleohungaricus*.

Homo neanderthalensis

H. neanderthalensis lived from about 250,000 to as recent as 30,000 years ago. Also proposed as *Homo sapiens neanderthalensis*: there is ongoing debate over whether the 'Neanderthal Man' was a separate species, *Homo neanderthalensis*, or a subspecies of *H. sapiens*. While the debate remains unsettled, evidence from mitochondrial

DNA and Y-chromosomal DNA sequencing indicates that little or no gene flow occurred between *H. neanderthalensis* and *H. sapiens*, and, therefore, the two were separate species. In 1997, Dr. Mark Stoneking, then an associate professor of anthropology at Pennsylvania State University, stated: "These results [based on mitochondrial DNA extracted from Neanderthal bone] indicate that Neanderthals did not contribute mitochondrial DNA to modern humans... Neanderthals are not our ancestors." Subsequent investigation of a second source of Neanderthal DNA supported these findings. However, supporters of the multiregional hypothesis point to recent studies indicating non-African nuclear DNA heritage dating to one mya, although the reliability of these studies have been questioned.

Homo rhodesiensis, and the Gawis cranium

- *H. rhodesiensis*, estimated to be 300,000–125,000 years old, most current experts believe Rhodesian Man to be within the group of Homo heidelbergensis though other designations such as Archaic Homo sapiens and Homo sapiens rhodesiensis have also been proposed.
- In February 2006 a fossil, the Gawis cranium, was found which might possibly be a species intermediate between *H. erectus* and *H. sapiens* or one of many evolutionary dead ends. The skull from Gawis, Ethiopia, is believed to be 500,000–250,000 years old. Only summary details are known, and no peer reviewed studies have been released by the finding team. Gawis man's facial features suggest its being either an intermediate species and an example of a "Bodo man" female.

Homo sapiens

H. sapiens ("sapiens" means wise or intelligent) has lived from about 250,000 years ago to the present. Between 400,000 years ago and the second interglacial period in the Middle Pleistocene, around 250,000 years ago, the trend in cranial expansion and the elaboration of stone tool technologies developed, providing evidence for a transition from *H. erectus* to *H. sapiens*. The direct evidence suggests there was a migration of *H. erectus* out of Africa, then a further speciation of *H. sapiens* from *H. erectus* in Africa (there is little evidence that this speciation occurred elsewhere). Then a subsequent migration within and out of Africa eventually replaced the earlier dispersed *H. erectus*. This migration and origin theory is usually referred to as the single-origin theory. However, the current evidence does not *preclude* multiregional speciation, either. This is a hotly debated area in paleoanthropology.

Current research has established that human beings are genetically highly homogenous, that is the DNA of individuals is more alike than usual for most species, which may have resulted from their relatively recent evolution or the Toba catastrophe. Distinctive genetic characteristics have arisen, however, primarily as the result of small groups of people moving into new environmental circumstances. Such small groups are initially highly inbred, allowing the relatively rapid transmission of traits favorable to the new environment. These adapted traits are a very small component of the *Homo sapiens* genome and include such outward "racial" characteristics as skin color and nose form in addition to internal characteristics such as the ability to breathe more efficiently in high altitudes.

H. sapiens idaltu, from Ethiopia, lived from about 160,000 years ago. It is the oldest known anatomically modern human.

Homo floresiensis

H. floresiensis, which lived about 100,000–12,000 years ago has been nicknamed *hobbit* for its small size, probably a result of insular (island) dwarfism. *H. floresiensis* is intriguing both for its size and its age, being a concrete example of a recent species of the genus *Homo* that exhibits derived traits not shared with modern humans. In other words, *H. floresiensis* share a common ancestor with modern humans, but split from the modern human lineage and followed a distinct evolutionary path. The main find was a skeleton believed to be a woman of about 30 years of age. Found in 2003 it has been dated to approximately 18,000 years old. Her brain size was only 380 cm^3 (which can be considered small even for a chimpanzee). She was only 1 meter in height.

However, there is an ongoing debate over whether *H. floresiensis* is indeed a separate species. Some scientists presently believe that *H. floresiensis* was a modern *H. sapiens* suffering from pathological dwarfism. This hypothesis is supported in part, because the modern humans who live on Flores, the island where the skeleton was found, are pygmies. This coupled with pathological dwarfism could indeed create a hobbit-like human. The other major attack on *H. floresiensis* is that it was found with tools only associated with *H. sapiens*.

Use of Tools

Using tools is not only a sign of intelligence, it also may have acted as a stimulus for human evolution. Over the past 3 or 2 million years, human brain size has increased threefold. A brain needs a lot of energy: the brain of modern man uses about 5 Watts (about 400 kilo calories per day), one fifth of total human energy consumption. Early hominoids, like apes, were essentially plant eaters (fruit, leaves, roots), their diet only occasionally supplemented by meat (often from scavenging). However, plant food in general yields considerably less energy and nutritive value than meat. Therefore, being able to hunt for large animals, which was only possible by using tools such as spears, made it possible for humans to sustain larger and more complex brains, which in turn allowed them to develop yet more intelligent and efficient tools.

Precisely when early man started to use tools is difficult to determine, because the more primitive these tools are (for example, sharp-edged stones) the more difficult it is to decide whether they are natural objects or human artifacts. There is some evidence that the australopithecines (4 mya) may have used broken bones as tools, but this is debated.

Stone tools

Stone tools are first attested around 2.6 million years ago, when *H. habilis* in Eastern Africa used so-called pebble tools, choppers made out of round pebbles that had been split by simple strikes. This marks the beginning of the Paleolithic, or Old Stone Age; its end is taken to be the end of the last Ice Age, around 10,000 years ago. The Paleolithic is subdivided into the Lower Paleolithic (Early Stone Age, ending around 350,000–300,000 years ago), the Middle Paleolithic (Middle Stone Age, until 50,000–30,000 years ago), and the Upper Paleolithic.

The period from 700,000–300,000 years ago is also known as the Acheulean, when *H. ergaster* (or *erectus*) made large stone hand-axes out of flint and quartzite, at first quite rough (Early Acheulian), later "retouched" by additional, more subtle strikes at the sides of the flakes. After 350,000

BP (Before Present) the more refined so-called Levallois technique was developed. It consisted of a series of consecutive strikes, by which scrapers, slicers ("racloirs"), needles, and flattened needles were made. This speed-up of cultural change seems connected with the arrival of modern humans, *homo sapiens*. As human culture advanced, different populations of humans began to create novelty in existing technologies. Artifacts such as fish hooks, buttons and bone needles begin to show signs of variation among different population of humans, something that had not been seen in human cultures prior to 50,000 BP. Typically, *neanderthalensis* populations are found with technology similar to other contemporary *neanderthalensis* populations.

Theoretically, modern human behavior is taken to include four ingredient capabilities: abstract thinking (concepts free from specific examples), planning (taking steps to achieve a farther goal), innovation (finding new solutions), and symbolic behaviour (such as images, or rituals). Among concrete examples of modern human behaviour, anthropologists include specialization of tools, use of jewelry and images (such as cave drawings), organization of living space, rituals (for example, burials with grave gifts), specialized hunting techniques, exploration of less hospitable geographical areas, and barter trade networks. Debate continues whether there was indeed a "revolution" leading to modern man ("the big bang of human consciousness"), or a more gradual evolution.

Notable Human Evolution Researchers

- James Burnett, Lord Monboddo, most famous today as a founder of modern comparative historical linguistics
- Henry McHenry, specializes in studies of human

evolution, the origins of bipedality, and paleoanthropology

- Svante Pääbo, a biologist specializing in evolutionary genetics
- Jeffrey H. Schwartz, an American physical anthropologist and professor of biological anthropology
- Erik Trinkaus, a prominent paleoanthropologist and expert on Neanderthal biology and human evolution
- Milford H. Wolpoff, a paleoanthropologist
- Charles Darwin, an English naturalist who documented considerable evidence that species originate through evolutionary change
- J.B.S. Haldane, a British geneticist and evolutionary biologist
- Leonard Shlain, a surgeon and author of three books
- Richard Dawkins, a British ethologist, evolutionary biologist who has promoted a gene-centered view of evolution.
- Sir Alister Hardy, a British zoologist, who first hypothesised the aquatic ape theory of human evolution.

II

TIMELINE OF EVOLUTION

This timeline of the evolution of life outlines the major events in the development of life on the planet Earth. For a thorough explanatory context, see the history of Earth, and geologic time scale. The dates given in this article are estimates based on scientific evidence.

In biology, evolution is the process by which populations of organisms acquire and pass on novel traits from generation to generation. Its occurrence over large stretches of time explains the origin of new species and ultimately the vast diversity of the biological world. Contemporary species are related to each other through common descent, products of evolution and speciation over billions of years.

Basic Timeline

The basic timeline is a 4.6 billion year old Earth, with approximately:

- 4 billion years of simple cells (prokaryotes),
- 3 billion years of photosynthesis,
- 2 billion years of complex cells (eukaryotes),
- 1 billion years of multicellular life,
- 600 million years of simple animals,
- 570 million years of arthropods (ancestors of insects, arachnids and crustaceans)
- 550 million years of complex animals
- 500 million years of fish and proto-amphibians,
- 475 million years of land plants,
- 400 million years of insects and seeds,
- 360 million years of amphibians,
- 300 million years of reptiles,
- 200 million years of mammals,
- 150 million years of birds,
- 130 million years of flowers,
- 65 million years since the non-avian dinosaurs died out and

- 2 million years since humans started looking like they do today.

For a list of ancestors common to humans and other living species, see The Ancestor's Tale.

Detailed timeline

In the tables below:

- "Ma" = "million years ago"
- "ka" = "thousand years ago"

Hadean eon

3800 Ma and earlier.

Date	*Event*
4567.17 Ma	The planet Earth forms from the accretion disc revolving around the young Sun.
4533 Ma	The planet Earth and the planet Theia collide, sending countless moonlets into orbit around the young Earth. These moonlets eventually coalesce to form the Moon. The gravitational pull of the new Moon stabilises the Earth's fluctuating axis of rotation and sets up the conditions for the formation of life.
4100 Ma	The surface of the Earth cools enough for the crust to solidify. The atmosphere and the oceans form.
4000 Ma	Information in this section has not been verified against sources and may

	not be reliable.Please check for inaccuracies and modify as needed, citing the sources against which it was checked.The earliest life appears, possibly derived from self-reproducing RNA molecules. The replication of these organisms requires resources like energy, space, and smaller building blocks, which soon become limited, resulting in competition. Natural selection favors those molecules which are more efficient at replication. DNA molecules then take over as the main replicators. They soon develop inside enclosing membranes which provide a stable physical and chemical environment conducive to their replication: proto-cells. At this time, the atmosphere does not contain any free oxygen.
3900 Ma	Late Heavy Bombardment: peak rate of impact events upon the Earth, Moon, Mars, Venus and Mercury by asteroids and comets (planetesimals). This constant disturbance may encourage life to evolve. It is thought that these impacts cause the oceans to boil away completely, more than once; yet life persists. Cells resembling prokaryotes appear. These first organisms are chemoautotrophs: they use carbon dioxide as a carbon source and oxidize inorganic materials to

extract energy. Later, prokaryotes evolve glycolysis, a set of chemical reactions that free the energy of organic molecules such as glucose. Glycolysis generates ATP molecules as short-term energy currency, and ATP continue to be used in almost all organisms, unchanged, to this day.

Archean eon

3800 Ma - 2500 Ma

3500 Ma	Lifetime of the last universal ancestor; the split between the bacteria and the archaea occurs. Bacteria develop primitive forms of photosynthesis which at first do not produce oxygen. These organisms generate ATP by exploiting a proton gradient, a mechanism still used in virtually all organisms.
3000 Ma	Photosynthesizing cyanobacteria evolve; they use water as a reducing agent, thereby producing oxygen as waste product. The oxygen initially oxidizes dissolved iron in the oceans, creating iron ore. The oxygen concentration in the atmosphere subsequently rises, acting as a poison for many bacteria. The moon is still very close to the earth and causes tides 1000 feet high. The earth is

continually wracked by hurricane force winds. These extreme mixing influences are thought to stimulate evolutionary processes.

Proterozoic eon

2500 Ma - 542 Ma

2500 Ma — Some bacteria evolve the ability to utilize oxygen to more efficiently use the energy from organic molecules such as glucose. Virtually all organisms using oxygen employ the same set of reactions, the citric acid cycle and oxidative phosphorylation. The "runaway icehouse" effect results in the Huronian glaciation (2500–2100 Ma).

2100 Ma — More complex cells appear: the eukaryotes, the closest relatives of whom are probably the archaea. Eukaryotes contain various organelles with diverse functions, probably derived from the co-evolution of symbiotic communities of prokaryotes. The most dramatic examples are mitochondria, which use oxygen to extract energy from organic molecules and appear similar to today's *Rickettsia*. Many eukaryotes also have chloroplasts, organelles which originated from cyanobacteria and similar organisms, which derive energy from light and synthesize organic molecules.

1200 Ma	Sexual reproduction evolves, leading to faster evolution. While most life still exists in oceans and lakes, some cyanobacteria may already live in moist soil by this time.
1000 Ma	Multicellular organisms appear: initially colonial algae, and later seaweeds, living in the oceans.
900 Ma	The choanoflagellates develop. These protists are considered the ancestors of the entire animal kingdom, and specifically the direct ancestors of the sponges: the choanocytes ("collar cells") of sponges (and a few other animal groups, such as flatworms) have the same basic structure as choanoflagellates, and DNA evidence suggests a close relationship between the two. The modern species proterospongia, consisting of choanoflagellates that live in colonies and exhibit primitive cell specialization for different tasks, is likely very similar to the ancient ancestor species that would have bridged the gap between choanoflagellates and sponges, and thereby between protozoa and all metazoa (multicellular animals).

1000–750 Ma	One of the first known supercontinents, Rodinia, forms, and then breaks apart again.
950–780 Ma	Sturtian ice age, a time of multiple near-global glaciations, with periods oscillating between a Snowball Earth and a greenhouse Earth.
900 Ma	There are 481 18-hour days in a year. The rotation of the Earth has gradually slowed ever since.
750–580 Ma	According to the Snowball Earth hypothesis, the Precambrian Varangian ice age is so severe that the Earth's oceans freeze over completely; only in the tropics do oceans remain liquid. This is the last big freeze, and afterwards, evolution begins to accelerate.
600 Ma	Sponges (Porifera), the earliest multicellular animals, develop from cell colonies. Sponges are the simplest and most primitive animals, having partially-differentiated tissues but no muscles, nerves, internal organs, or capacity for locomotion. JellyfishFollowing sponges, Cnidaria (jellyfish, etc.), Ctenophora, and other unidentified multicellular animals appear in the oceans. Cnidaria and Ctenophora are some of the earliest creatures to have neurons, in the form

of a simple net, with no central nervous system. They possess muscular tissue and digestive systems with mouths. Unlike sponges, these animals have structured bodies with organs and radial symmetry.FlatwormFlatworms (Platyhelminthes), the earliest animals to have a rudimentary brain and the simplest animals with bilateral symmetry, develop. They are also the simplest animals to have organs that form from three germ layers (triploblasty). There are still no organisms with a true circulatory or respiratory system.

570 Ma Arthropods begin to appear. Praecambridium is one of the first to appear.

The Ozone layer forms, allowing for the first major excursions onto the land. The second supercontinent, Pannotia, forms, then breaks up by 540 Ma.

Phanerozoic eon

542 Ma - present

Consists of three eras:

- Paleozoic era (542 Ma - 251.0 Ma)
- Mesozoic era (251.0 Ma - 65.5 Ma)
- Cenozoic era (65.5 Ma - present)

Paleozoic era
542 Ma - 251.0 Ma

542–530 Ma — The Cambrian explosion, a rapid set of evolutionary changes, creates all the major body plans (phyla) of modern animals. The cause of this huge expansion in the variety of life forms is still a matter of scientific debate. Arthropoda, represented by an abundance of trilobites, is the dominant phylum. *Anomalocaris* is a predator up to 2 meters in length. The worm-like organisms develop more highly specialized and advanced structures, such as the circulatory system of acorn worms, which features a heart that also functions as a kidney. Acorn worms have a gill-like structure, similar to that of primitive fish, used for breathing. Acorn worms are thus sometimes said to be a link between vertebrates and invertebrates.Pikaia*Pikaia*, a small swimmer and the earliest-known animal with a notochord, is believed to be the ancestor of all chordates and vertebrates. The lancelet, a species still alive today, retains some of the features of the primitive chordates, and resembles the *Pikaia* in many ways. The conodont is an "eel-shaped animal of 4–20 cm long" with a pair of huge eyes and a complex basket of teeth.The first known footprints on land date to 530 Ma, indicating that early animal explorations may have predated the development of terrestrial plants.

505 Ma — The first vertebrates appear: the ostracoderms, jawless fish (Agnatha) such as *Haikouichthys* and *Myllokunmingia*. They have cartilaginous internal skeletons, and lack the paired (pectoral and pelvic) fins of more advanced prehistoric fish. They are precusors of the Osteichthyes (bony fish), and are related to present-day lampreys and hagfishes.

488 Ma — The first of the seven major extinction events over geological time occurs at the Cambrian-Ordovician transition.

475 Ma — The first primitive plants move onto land, having evolved from green algae living along the edges of lakes. They are accompanied by fungi, and very likely plants and fungi work symbiotically together; lichens exemplify such a symbiosis but however some scientists believe that the molecular clock is evidence for a much earlier appearance of land plants and fungi and believe that fungi 1000 Ma in the tonian period of the Neoproterozoic era and that land

plants appeared somewhere around 700 ma in the Cryogenian era of the Neoprotrozoic.

450 Ma Arthropods, with an exoskeleton that provides support and prevents water loss, are the first animals to move onto land. Among the first are Myriapoda (millipedes and centipedes), later followed by spiders and scorpions. Over the next ten million years, the two Ordovician-Silurian extinction events occur. Taken together, these constitute the second mass extinction event.Soon after, the first of the jawed fishes, Placodermi, develop. Their jaws evolve from the first of their gill arches. Their head and thorax are covered by articulated armored plates, while the rest of the body is scaled or naked.

410 Ma First *Coelacanth* appears; this order of animals had been thought to have no extant members, until living specimens were discovered in 1938. It is often referred to as a living fossil.

400 Ma The first insects evolve, the wingless silverfish, springtails (no longer considered insects), and bristletails. First sharks appear.

385 Ma Eusthenopteron, though still an ocean dweller, led to the line of tetrapods which would walk on land.

375 Ma *Tiktaalik* is a genus of sarcopterygian (lobe-finned) fishes from the late Devonian with many tetrapod-like features.

370 Ma *Cladoselache*, a shark, is a high-speed predator.

365 Ma The Late Devonian extinction is the third mass extinction. New insect species evolve on land and in fresh water from the myriapods.PanderichthysSome lobe-finned fish (Sarcopterygii) develop legs and give rise to early four-limbed tetrapods: Ichthyostega, Acanthostega and *Pederpes finneyae*. Initially aquatic, dwelling in shallow, swampy freshwater habitats, these fishes use their fins as paddles to assist in navigating shallow waters choked with plants and detritus—the likely origin of front limbs bending backward at the elbow and hind limbs bending forward at the knee. Eventually, these tetrapods use their rudimentary legs to move out onto land for brief periods, probably to hunt insects. Lungs and swim bladders evolve.Primitive tetrapods developed from a fish with a two-lobed brain in a flattened skull, a wide mouth, and a short snout, whose upward-facing eyes show that it was a bottom-dweller, and which had already developed adaptations

	of fins with fleshy bases and bones. The "living fossil" coelacanth is a related lobe-finned fish without these shallow-water adaptations. Amphibians today still retain many characteristics of the early tetrapods.
360 Ma	Plants evolve seeds, structures that protect plant embryos and enable plants to spread quickly on land. Creation of Woodleigh crater (100 km wide) and Siljan Ring (40 km wide, Dalarna, Sweden).
360–286 Ma	The golden age of sharks.
350-251 Ma	The Karoo Ice Age begins in the early Carboniferous and ends in the Permian. Advancing ice sheets in Gondwanaland are at first centered in Africa and South America, and later in India and Australia, due to polar wandering.
300 Ma	Pangaea before its break-up.The supercontinent Pangaea forms and will last for 120 million years; this is the last time all of the earth's continents fuse into one. Evolution of the amniotic egg gives rise to the Amniota, reptiles, who can reproduce on land. Insects evolve flight, and include a number of different orders (e.g. Palaeodictyoptera, Megasecoptera, Diaphanopterodea, and Protorthoptera) Dragonflies

and Protorthoptera) Dragonflies (Odonata) still resemble many of these early insects. Vast forests of clubmosses (lycopods), horsetails, and tree ferns cover the land; when these decay they will eventually form coal and oil. Gymnosperms begin to diversify widely. Cycads, plants resembling palms, first appear.

280 Ma — The Protodonatan dragonfly *Meganeura monyi* is among the biggest insects that ever lived, with a wingspan of about 2 feet. Vertebrates include many Temnospondyl, Anthrachosaur, and Lepospondyl amphibians and early anapsid and synapsid (e.g. *Edaphosaurus*) amniotes.

256 Ma — *Diictodon*, *Cistecephalus*, *Dicynodon*, *Lycaenops*, *Dinogorgon* and *Procynosuchus*, are a few of the many mammal-like reptiles known from South Africa and Russia. Pareiasaurs were large clumsy herbivores. The first Archosauriformes.

250 Ma — The Permian-Triassic extinction event wipes out about 90% of all animal species; this fourth extinction event is the most severe mass extinction known. *Lystrosaurus* is a common herbivore that survives the extinction event. The archosaurs split from other

reptiles. Teleosts evolve from among the Actinopterygii (ray-finned fish), and eventually become the dominant fish group. Atmospheric oxygen, at 10%, is one third of its former level, so animals with air sac breathing systems will do well (present-day bird respiration exemplifies the air sac system). Some spores of bacteria Bacillus strain 2-9-3 (*Sali bacillus marismortui*) are trapped in salt crystals known as halite in New Mexico. They are re-animated in AD 2000 and have multiplied rapidly to currently be the world's oldest living organism.

Mesozoic era
251.0 Ma - 65.5 Ma

220 Ma — *Eoraptor*, an early dinosaur.The climate is very dry, and dry-adapted organisms are favored: the archosaurs and the Gymnosperms. Archosaurs diversify into crocodilians, dinosaurs, and pterosaurs. From synapsids come the first mammal precursors, therapsids, and more specifically the eucynodonts. Initially, they stay small and shrew-like. All mammals have milk glands for their young, and they keep a constant body temperature. Also, one of a pair of autosomes acquires gene SRY (derived from the

SOX3 gene of the X chromosome) to become the Y chromosome, which has been decreasing in length since. Gymnosperms (mostly conifers) are the dominant land plants. Plant eaters will grow to huge sizes during the dominance of the gymnosperms to have space for large guts to digest the poor food offered by gymnosperms.

208-144 Ma — Second major spread of sharks.

200 Ma — Fifth mass extinction event occurs at the Triassic-Jurassic transition. Marine reptiles include Ichthyosaurs and Plesiosaurs. Ammonites and belemnites flourish. Dinosaurs survive the extinction and grow to large size, but the thecodonts, or "socket-toothed" reptiles, die out. Modern amphibians evolve: the Lissamphibia; including Anura (frogs), Urodela (salamanders), and Caecilia. Geminiviridae, a diverse group of viruses, are traceable to this epoch or earlier.

180 Ma — Pangaea's break-up.The supercontinent Pangaea begins to break up into several land masses. The largest is Gondwana, made up of the land masses which are now Antarctica, Australia, South America, Africa, and India. Antarctica is still a land of forests. North America and

	Eurasia are still joined, forming the Northern supercontinent, Laurasia. Speciation occurs due to the water barriers created by the breakup.The first true mammals appear, from mammaliform ancestors.
164 Ma	The oldest swimming mammal, Castorocauda lutrasimilis, is the immediate predecessor of modern mammals such as the platypus and echidna (i.e. monotremes, consitituting the most primitive mammalian order).
160 Ma	3 metres long, *Guanlong wucaii*—meaning *crested dragon from the five colours*, Xinjiang province in northwestern China, is the oldest Tyrannosaur.
150 Ma	Giant dinosaurs are common and diverse—*Brachiosaurus*, *Apatosaurus*, *Stegosaurus*, *Allosaurus*, along with smaller forms like *Ornitholestes* and *Othnielosaurus*. Birds evolve from theropod dinosaurs. *Archaeopteryx* is an ancestor of birds, with claws, feathers but no beak.
135 Ma	New dinosaurs *Iguanodon*, *Hylaeosaurus*, etc., appear after extinction of Jurassic forms. *Microraptor gui*, a 77 cm long dinosaur in Liaoning, Northeast China, has bird-like feathered wings on 4 limbs.

133 Ma	*Shenzhouraptor sinensis*, a primitive bird found in the Yixian Formation of north-eastern China, eats seeds. The bird has large, strong wings, and also had a long, bony tail, like many dinosaurs.
130 Ma	Angiosperm plants evolve flowers, structures that attract insects and other animals to spread pollen. This innovation of the angiosperms causes a major burst of animal evolution and co-evolution.
128 Ma	One early tyrannosaur is *Dilong paradoxus* in Lioning Province of China. Has feathers and a small body of 5 feet (1.5 m) long.
125 Ma	*Eomaia scansoria*, a eutherian mammal, which leads to the formation of modern placental mammals. It looks like a modern dormouse, climbing small shrubs in Liaoning, China. The parrot-beaked *Psittacosaurus* is the ancestor of the later horned dinosaurs.
123 Ma	*Sinornithosaurus millenii* is a dinosaur in Liaoning, China that has primitive feathers not used for flight. Other dinosaurs with feathers are *Sinosauropteryx* (most primitive feathers, simplest tubular structures) and *Changchanornis*. Other dinosaurs include *Polacanthus* (armoured

	herbivore) and *Eotyrannus* (early tyrannosaur). Evolution of birds has gone underway, with several different lineages existing (e.g. *Confuciusornis* and 'Yanornis*)*.
110 Ma	*Sarcosuchus imperator*, eight metric tons, 12 m long, head 2 m long, largest crocodile. Carnivorous dinosaurs included the "raptor" *Deinonychus* and sail-backed semi-aquatic spinosaurs, herbivores include the tallest known sauropod *Sauroposeidon proteles*, as well as the bulbous-nosed iguanodont *Altirhinus* (ancestral to duck-bills) and the armoured *Sauropelta*. *Gansus yumenensis*, the earliest known essentially modern bird, lives in today's China.
100 Ma	The giant theropod dinosaurs *Carcharodontosaurus* and *Giganotosaurus* are even bigger than *Tyrannosaurus*.
88 Ma	Breakup of Indo-Malagasy land mass.
80 Ma	Many kinds of sauropod, duck billed, horned and meat-eating dinosaurs; half of all known dinosaur species are from the last 30 MY of the Mesozoic, after the rise of the angiosperms. India starts moving to Eurasia.
75 Ma	*Oviraptor* was one of the most bird-

75 Ma	*Oviraptor* was one of the most bird-like of the non-avian dinosaurs. Last common ancestor of humans and mice. The Hesperornithes and Ichthyornithes, extinct birds with teeth, roamed the oceans of the Northern Hemisphere.
67 Ma	*Vegavis iaai*, the oldest known bird assignable to a group still extant today, lives on the shores of Antarctica. It is a presbyornithid, a kind of wading goose.

Cenozoic era
65.5 Ma - present

65 Ma	An asteroid impact probably wiped out half of all animals species 65 million years ago. Other life forms became extinct as well.The Cretaceous-Tertiary extinction event (sixth extinction event) wipes out about half of all animal species including all non-avian dinosaurs, probably because of a cooling of the climate precipitated by the giant impact of an asteroid: iridium powder from the asteroid forms a layer that covers the whole Earth. Creation of the Chicxulub Crater (170 km across, now half-submerged off the Yucatan peninsula of Mexico). Without the presence of the giant and diurnal

dinosaurs, mammals can increase in diversity and size. Some will later return back to the sea (whales, sirenians, seals) and others will evolve flight (bats). A group of small, nocturnal and arboreal, insect-eating mammals called the Archonta branches into what will be the primates, treeshrews, and bats. Primates have binocular vision and grasping digits, features that help them to jump from one tree branch to another. One example of a proto-primate is *Plesiadapis* which is extinct by 45 million years ago. Except the Neornithes lineage which exists today, all birds become extinct in the catastrophe.

60 Ma *Creodont*, meat eater, northern hemisphere, extinct by 5.2 million years ago, possible ancestor of Miacids. Legumes are first recorded in the fossil record

55 Ma *Carpolestes simpsoni*, a primate-like mammal.Australia breaks away from Antarctica. Proto-primates first appear in North America, Asia, and Europe. One example is *Carpolestes simpsoni* at Clarks Fork Basin of Wyoming. It has grasping digits but no forward facing eyes. Another (earliest?) euprimate *Teilhardina asiatica* (Hunan, China) is mouse-

	sized, diurnal, and has small eyes. An ancestor of the Shortfin mako shark probably gives rise to the lineage of the Great White Shark, but not the Megalodon.
50 Ma	The evolution of the horse starts with *Hyracotherium*: the size of a fox with large nails instead of hoofs. Ancestor of whales (which include dolphins), *Ambulocetus natans* (Pakistan) probably walks on land like the modern sea lion and swims like modern otters. It has webbed feet that give it added power when swimming, and still hears directly from its ears. *Pezosiren portelli*, ancestor of modern manatees, walks like a hippo and swims like an otter. Miacids include *Miacis*, a five-clawed ancestor of all dogs, cats, bears, raccoon, fox, hyena, jackal, civet; it is a meat-eating, weasel-like tree climber.
48.5 Ma	*Gastornis geiselensis* (Europe, USA), a carnivorous bird 1.75 m tall, is a top predator
46.5 Ma	*Rodhocetus*, ancestor of whale, successor to *Ambulocetus*, no longer needs to drink fresh water.
43 Ma	Earliest elephant, *Moeritherium* (Egypt): 1 m tall, size of a large pig,

eats soft, juicy plants. It has a long nose, but no trunk nor tusks.

40 Ma Primates (order) diverge into suborders Strepsirrhini (lemurs and lorises) and Haplorrhini (tarsiers, monkeys and apes); the latter is diurnal and herbivorous.

37 Ma *Basilosaurus*, up to 20 m long, snakelike ancestor of whales, has reduced but well-developed hind limbs. Hears from sounds transmitted to middle ears through vibrations from lower jaws. In Egypt's 'Whale Valley', what would later be the Wadi Hitan desert is underwater, teeming with *Basilosaurus isis* which had no blowhole but had to raise its head above water to breathe. Early ancestors of strepsirrhines primate appear in the Egyptian desert, *Biretia fayumensis* and *Biretia megalopsis*..

35 Ma Grasses evolve from among the angiosperms.

34 Ma Cynodictis, or dawn dog, appears in North America. Canids will eventually colonize the world.

30 Ma Haplorrhini (suborder) splits into infraorders Platyrrhini (New World monkeys) and Catarrhini (Old World primates). New World monkeys have prehensile tails and males are color

	blind. They supposedly migrated to South America on a raft of vegetation across the Atlantic ocean (circa 4,500km). Catarrhines stay in Africa as the two continents drift further apart. One ancestor of catarrhines might be *Aegyptopithecus*. Haplorrhines: *Bugtipithecus inexpectans*, *Phileosimias kamali* and *Phileosimias brahuiorum*, similar to today's lemurs, live in rainforests on Bugti Hills of central Pakistan. Ancestor of all cats, 9 kg *Proailurus*, lives in trees in Europe, goes extinct 20 million years ago.
27.5 Ma	*Indricothere*, rhino relative, 4.5 m tall, tallest mammal on land, lives in Mongolia.
27 Ma	The Phorusrhacidae ("Terror birds"), up to 2.5 m tall, are among the top-level carnivores in the Americas. They went extinct only 2 million years ago.
25 Ma	Catarrhini males gain color vision but lose the pheromone pathway. Catarrhini splits into 2 superfamilies, Old World monkeys (Cercopithecoidea) and apes (Hominoidea). The Old World primates do not have prehensile tails (e.g. Baboon); some do not have tails at all. All hominoids are without tails.

22 Ma — India colliding with the Cimmerian coast.India collides with Asia, causing the rise of Himalaya and the Tibetan plateau. Cut off from the humidity, Central Asia becomes a desert. Appearance of *deinotherium*, ancient elephant, extinct by 2 million years ago. Evolving from an animal that looks part dog, part bear and part raccoon, the dawn bear (*Ursavus elmensis*) is the ancestor of all bears living today. It is the size of a fox, hunts in the tree tops, and supplements a diet of meat with plant material and insects. The first group, the *Ailuropodinae*, follows a plant-based diet, branches off, and only one member, the giant panda (*Ailuropoda melanoleuca*), survives today.

20 Ma — The African plate collides with Asia. *Cynodictis*, ancestor of dogs, has a shortened fifth claw which foreshadows the dewclaw (vestigial) of modern dogs. They look like the modern day civet and have feet and toes suited for running. The two superfamilies of carnivores (canines and felines) are distinct by this time. *Gomphotherium*, ancient elephant.

19 Ma — *Megatherium americanum* (giant sloth, 6 m long, extinct 8000 years

	ago) and *Argentavis magnificens* (the largest bird ever to fly, wingspan some 7 meters or more) are among the gigantic animals that roam South America.
16 Ma	*Squalodon* shows early echolocation of whales. *Megalodon* is a gigantic shark the size of a bus; it has a long reign and disappears suddenly about 1.6 Ma.
15 Ma	Apes from Africa migrate to Eurasia to become gibbons (lesser apes) and orangutans. Human ancestors speciate from the ancestors of the gibbon. Orangutans, gorillas and chimpanzees are great apes. Humans are hominins.
13 Ma	Human ancestors speciate from the ancestors of the orangutan. A relative of orangutans: *Lufengpithecus chiangmuanensis* (Northern Thailand). *Pierolapithecus catalaunicus*, Spain, possibly common ancestor of great apes and humans.
10 Ma	The climate begins to dry; savannas and grasslands take over the forests. Monkeys proliferate, and the apes go into decline. Human ancestors speciate from the ancestors of the gorillas. This is the heyday of the horses as they spread throughout the Northern hemisphere. After 10 Ma

	they decline in the face of competition from the artiodactyls. Tomarctus, ancestor of dogs, is an extremely dog like animal.
7 Ma	Biggest primate *Gigantopithecus* is 2 m tall and lives in China (*Gigantopithecus blacki*), Vietnam, and northern India (*Gigantopithecus bilaspurensis*). Extinct by 300,000 years ago.
5.6 Ma	Drying up of the Mediterranean Sea (the Messinian Event).
5 Ma	Volcanoes erupt and create the small area of land that joins North and South America. Mammals from North America move South and cause extinction of mammals there. Human ancestors speciate from the ancestors of the chimpanzees. The latest common ancestor is *Sahelanthropus tchadensis* (Chad, Sahara, west of Rift Valley). The earliest in the human branch is *Orrorin tugenensis* (Millennium Man, Kenya). Chimpanzees and humans share 98% of DNA: biochemical similarities are so great that their hemoglobin molecules differ by only one amino acid. One group of chimps can have more genetic diversity than all of the six billion humans alive today, due to later population bottlenecking on

	the human lineage. Both chimpanzees and humans have a larynx that repositions during the first two years of life to a spot between the pharynx and the lungs, indicating that the common ancestors have this feature, a precursor of speech.
4.8 Ma	Chimpanzee size hominin genus, *Ardipithecus* walks upright
3.7 Ma	Some *Australopithecus afarensis* leave footprints on volcanic ash in Laetoli, Kenya (Northern Tanzania).
3.5 Ma	Orangutans diverge into Bornean (*Pongo pygmaeus*) and Sumatran (*Pongo abelii*) sub-species. Great white sharks appear.
3 Ma	AustralopithecusThe bipedal australopithecines (early hominins) evolve in the savannas of Africa being hunted by *Dinofelis*. Species include *Australopithecus africanus*, *Australopithecus bosei*. Other genera include *Kenyanthropus platyops*. Gorillas die out on the South bank of the Congo River. North and South America become joined, allowing migration of animals. Modern horses, *Equus* first appear. *Deinotherium* (4 m tall), is a gigantic cousin of the elephant, with downward pointing tusks in the lower jaw.

2.5 Ma	*Smilodon* (Saber-toothed cat) appears.
2.2 Ma	Gorillas diverge into the Western lowland (*Gorilla gorilla*) and Eastern (*Gorilla beringei*) sub-species.
2 Ma	*Homo habilis* (handy man) uses primitive stone tools (choppers) in Tanzania. Probably lives with *Paranthropus robustus*. Emergence of Broca's area (speech region of modern human brain). *Homo* species are meat-eating while *Paranthropus* eats plants and termites. Some chimpanzees (*Pan troglodytes*) at the Southern part of the Congo River branch off to form the Bonobos (*Pan paniscus*/pigmy chimps). Bonobos live in female dominated society. Saber Tooth moves from North America to South America.
1.8 Ma	*Homo erectus* evolves in Africa and migrates to other continents, primarily South Asia. A large-scale extinction of marine life is triggered by some event, possibly a supernova. Many seabirds, which have dominated the shores and coastal waters for some 20 million years, become extinct; marine mammals diversify and take their place.
1.75 Ma	Dmanisi man/*Homo georgicus* (Georgia, Russia), tiny brain came from Africa, with *Homo erectus* and

Homo habilis characteristics. An individual spent the last years of his life with only one tooth by depending on the kindness and compassion of others to obtain sufficient sustenance. The glyptodon, a giant armadillo the size of a Volkswagen Beetle, lives in southern Peru.

1.6 Ma — Biggest marsupials: Appearance of Giant Short-faced Kangaroo (*Procoptodon goliah*) in Australia, extinct by 40,000 years ago. At 2 m to 3 m tall and weighing 200 kg to 300 kg, it is the largest kangaroo ever known. Wombat-like *Diprotodon optatum*, 2,800 kg, 3 m long, Australia, extinct by 45,000 years ago.

1.5 Ma — Marsupial lion (*Thylacoleo carnifex* or Leo) appears in Australia and goes extinct by 46,000 years ago.

1 Ma — Genus *Canis* (coyotes, jackals, wolves, dingoes, domestic dogs) develops as a branch from *Tomarctus*. The gray fox, *Urocyon cinereoargenteus* is the most primitive canid still alive today.

800 ka — Gray Wolf (*Canis lupus*) moves to Arctic North America.

780 ka — The Earth's last (most recent) geomagnetic reversal.

700 ka — Common genetic ancestor of humans and Neanderthals.

500 ka	*Homo erectus* (Choukoutien, China) uses charcoal to control fire, though they may not know how to create or start it.
400 ka	Eastern gorillas (*Gorilla beringei*) diverge into the eastern lowland (*G. beringei graueri*) and mountain (*G. beringei beringei*) sub-species. Giant deer *Megaloceros giganteus*, Ireland; the antlers together span about 3.6 m or larger, extinct by 9.5 ka.
355 ka	Three 1.5 m tall *Homo heidelbergensis* scramble down Roccamonfina volcano in Southern Italy, leaving the earliest known *Homo* footprints, which were made before the powdery volcanic ash solidified.
250 ka	The Polar Bear evolves from an isolated high latitude population of Brown Bears.
195 ka	Omo1, Omo2 (Ethiopia, Omo river) are the earliest known *Homo sapiens*.
160 ka	*Homo sapiens* (*Homo sapiens idaltu*) in Ethiopia, Awash River, Herto village, practise mortuary rituals and butcher hippos. Their dead bodies are later covered by volcanic rocks.
150 ka	"Mitochondrial Eve" lives in Africa. She is the last female ancestor common to all mitochondrial lineages in humans alive today.

130 ka	*Homo neanderthalensis* (Neanderthal man) evolves from *Homo heidelbergensis* and lives in Europe and the Middle East, buries the dead and cares for the sick. Has hyoid bone (60,000 yrs ago, Kebara cave, Israel), used for speech in modern humans. (Today humans use roughly 6000 spoken languages). Uses spear, probably for stabbing rather than throwing. FOXP2 gene appears (associated with the development of speech).
100 ka	The first anatomically modern humans (*Homo sapiens*) appear in Africa by this time or earlier; they derive from *Homo heidelbergensis*. *Homo sapiens* (humans) live in South Africa (Klasies River Caves) and Palestine (Qafzeh and Es Skhul), probably alongside Neanderthals. Modern humans enter Asia via two routes: one North through the Middle East, and another further South from Ethiopia, via the Red Sea and southern Arabia. Mutation causes skin color changes in order to absorb optimal UV light for different geographical latitudes. Modern "race" formation begins. African populations remain more 'diverse' in their genetic makeup than all other humans, since only a subset of their population (and therefore only a subset of their

	diversity) leaves Africa. For example, mtDNA shows that an individual with English ancestors is more similar genetically to an individual with Japanese ancestors than are two individuals drawn from two African populations.
82.5 ka	Humans in Zaire fish using sharp blades spears made from animal bones.
82 ka	Humans in the Grotte des Pigeons, Taforalt, Morocco, colour with red ochre and pierce holes through sea shells (Nassarius) to make beads for personal adornment.
80 ka	Humans make bone harpoons in Katanda, Democratic Republic of Congo.
74 ka	Supervolcanoic eruption in Toba, Sumatra, Indonesia, possibly causes *Homo sapiens* population to crash to 2,000. Six years without a summer are followed by a 1,000 year ice-age. Volcanic ash up to 5 m deep covers India and Pakistan.
70 ka	The most recent ice age, the Wisconsin glaciation, begins. Humans in the Blombos cave in South Africa make tools from bones, show symbolic thinking by creating ochre paintings. They also collect and pierce holes

	through sea shells to make necklaces. Giant beavers (*Castoroides ohioensis*, Toronto, Canada) largest rodents, length up to 2.5 m, dies out 10,000 years ago.
60 ka	"Y-chromosomal Adam" lives in Africa. He is the last common male ancestor of all humans alive today.
50 ka	Modern humans expand from Asia to Australia (to become today's Indigenous Australians) and Europe. Expansion along the coasts happens faster than expansion inland. Woolly rhino (*Coelodonta antiquus*) in Britain.
40 ka	Cro-Magnon Humans paint and hunt mammoths in France. They have extraordinary cognitive powers equivalent to modern humans, which enable them to become predators/hunters at the top of the food chain. Megafauna extinction starts (continuing to current day); most large mammal species disappear, directly or indirectly due to the expanding human population.
32 ka	First sculpture found in Vogelherd, Germany. First (bird bone) flute found in France. Stone tools in Kota Tampan, Malaysia.

30 ka	Modern humans enter North America from Siberia in numerous waves, some later waves across the Bering land bridge, but early waves probably by island-hopping across the Aleutians. At least two of the first waves left few or no genetic descendants among Americans by the time Europeans arrive across the Atlantic Ocean. Humans reach Solomon Islands and Japan. Bow and arrows used in Sahara (grassland). Fired ceramic animal models made in Moravia (Czech Republic).
28 ka	Oldest known painting: in the Apollo 11 Rock Shelter, Namibia, Africa. A 20 cm-long, 3 cm-wide object found in Hohle Fels Cave near Ulm in the Swabian Jura in Germany is the earliest sculpted stone penis.
27 ka	*Neanderthals* die out leaving *Homo sapiens* and *Homo floresiensis* as the only living species of the genus *Homo*. In today's Czech Republic, humans invent textiles and press weaving patterns into pieces of clay before firing them.
25 ka	Throwing sticks for hunting animals made from mammoth tusk (Poland).
23 ka	Venus of Willendorf, a small statuette of a female figure, discovered at a

	Paleolithic site near Willendorf, Austria, dates from this era. First intentional growing of food plants by humans occurs in the Near East, but is not associated with land clearing or tillage.
20 ka	Humans leave foot and hand prints in Tibetan plateau. Oil lamps made from animal fats on shells used in caves in Grotte de la Mouthe, France. Bone needles used to sew animal hides. (Shandingdong Man, China). Microblade culture (Northern China). Mammoth bones used to build houses (Russia). Ishango Bone might be first example of mathematics.
18 ka	*Homo floresiensis* existed in the Liang Bua limestone cave on Flores, remote Indonesian island.
15 ka	The last Ice Age ends. Sea levels across the globe rise, flooding many coastal areas, and separating former mainland areas into islands. Japan separates from Asia mainland. Siberia separates from Alaska. Tasmania separates from Australia. Java island forms. Sarawak, Malaysia and Indonesia separate. The cave paintings of Lascaux and Altamira were produced. Sedentary hunter-gather societies develop in the

	Natufian culture of the Near East—an essential precursor to later agricultural societies.
14 ka	Megafauna extinction starts in the Americas.
11.5 ka	Extinction of the Sabertooth (*Smilodon*) and Merriam's Teratorn (the "thunderbird";;).
11 ka	Human population reaches 5 million. Extinction of *Homo floresiensis*. Extinction of woolly mammoth. Domestication of dogs (first domesticated animal) from Gray Wolf subspecies (*Canis lupus pallipes*). All modern dogs today (5 main groups, about 400 breeds) belong to a single subspecies *Canis lupus familiaris*.
10 ka	Humans in the Fertile Crescent of the Middle East develop agriculture. Plant domestication begins with cultivation of Neolithic founder crops. This process of food production, coupled later with the domestication of animals caused a massive increase in human population that has continued to the present. Jericho (modern Israel) settlement with about 19,000 people.
10 ka	Sahara is green with rivers, lakes, cattles, crocodiles and monsoons.

	Japan's hunter-gatherer Jômon culture creates world's earliest pottery. Humans reach Tierra del Fuego at the tip of South America, the last continental region to be inhabited by humans (excluding Antarctica).
8 ka	Common (Bread) wheat *Triticum aestivum* originates in southwest Asia due to hybridisation of emmer wheat with a goat-grass, *Aegilops tauschii*.
6.5 ka	Two rice species are domesticated: Asian rice *Oryza sativa* and African rice *Oryza glaberrima*.
3.5 ka	Humans in Mesoamerica develop the foundations of organized religion, with initiated priests overseeing rituals.
3 ka	Humans in Eurasia start using iron tools.
AD 1	Human population 150 million.
AD 1835	Human population 1 billion.
AD 1969	Humans walk on the moon.
AD 2007	Human population approaching 6.6 billion. Holocene extinction event continues (*commencing 30-40 ka*) with the observed rate of extinction rising dramatically in the last 50 years. Most biologists believe that we are at this

> moment at the beginning of a tremendously accelerated anthropogenic mass extinction. Wilson estimates that at current rates of human destruction of the biosphere, one-half of all species of life will be extinct in 100 years.

This is evident from the above timeline the we *Homo sapiens sapiens* have treded a long march from the very beginning to the present.

3

PHILOSOPHICAL AND THEOLOGICAL ANTHROPOLOGY

I

First of all, it must be remembered that philosophical anthropology is the philosophical discipline that seeks to unify the several empirical investigations and phenomenological explorations of human nature in an effort to understand human beings as both creatures of their environment and creators of their own values. Although the majority of philosophers throughout the history of philosophy can be said to have a distinctive "anthropology" that undergirds their thought, philosophical anthropology itself, as a *specific discipline* in philosophy, arose within the later modern period as an outgrowth from developing methods in philosophy, such as phenomenology and existentialism. The former, which draws its energy from methodical reflection of human experience from the philosopher's own personal experience, naturally aided the emergence of philosophical explorations of human nature and the human condition.

Max Scheler, a German phenomenologist, is known for his highly developed philosophical anthropology which defines the human being not so much as a "rational animal" (as has traditionally been the case since Aristotle) but essentially as a loving being. He breaks down the traditional hylomorphic conception of the human person, and describes the personal being with a tripartite structure of lived body, soul, and spirit. Love and hatred are not psychological emotions, but spiritual, intentional acts of the person, which he categorises as "intentional feelings." Other important philosophical anthropologists are Rene Girard, Helmuth Plessner, Arnold Gehlen, Paul Häberlin, and Hans-Eduard Hengstenberg.

II

THEOLOGY

Theologians use philosophical analysis and argument to understand, explain, test, critique, defend or promote any of a myriad of religious topics. Theology might be undertaken to help the theologian understand more truly his or her own religious tradition, understand more truly another religious tradition, make comparisons between religious traditions, defend a religious tradition, facilitate reform of a particular tradition, assist in the propagation of a religious tradition, or draw on the resources of a tradition to address some present situation or need, or for a variety of other reasons.

The word 'theology' has classical Greek origins, but was slowly given new senses when it was taken up in both Greek and Latin forms by Christian authors. It is the subsequent history of the term in Christian contexts, particularly in the Latin West, that lies behind most contemporary usage, but the term can now be used to speak of reasoned discourse within and about a variety of different religious traditions. Various aspects both of the process by which the discipline of 'theology' emerged in Christianity and the process by which the term was extended to other religions are highly controversial.

The word "theology" originated in Ancient Greece, but its meaning shifted as it was used (in Greek and in Latin) in European Christian thought in the Patristic period, the Middle Ages and Enlightenment, before being taken up more widely.

- The term *theologia* is used in Classical Greek literature, with the meaning "discourse on the gods or cosmology"
- Aristotle divided theoretical philosophy into *mathematice*, *phusike* and *theologike*, with the latter corresponding roughly to metaphysics, which for Aristotle included discussion of the nature of the divine.
- Drawing on Greek sources, the Latin writer Varro influentially distinguished three forms of such discourse: mythical (concerning the myths of the Greek gods), rational (philosophical analysis of the gods and of cosmology) and civil (concerning the rites and duties of public religious observance.
- Christian writers, working within the Hellenistic mould, began to use the term to describe their studies. It appears once in some biblical manuscripts, in the heading to the book of Revelation: *apokalupsis ioannou tou theologou*, "the revelation of John the *theologos*". There, however, the word refers not to John the "theologian" in the modern English sense of the word but -using a slightly different sense of the root *logos* meaning not "rational discourse" but "word" or "message" - one who speaks the words of God - *logoi tou theou*.
- Other Christian writers used this term with several different ranges of meaning.

Some Latin authors, such as Tertullian and Augustine followed Varro's threefold usage, described above.

- In patristic Greek sources, *theologia* could refer narrowly to devout and inspired knowledge of, and teaching about, the essential nature of God.
- In some medieval Greek and Latin sources, *theologia* (in the sense of "an account or record of the ways of God") could refer simply to the Bible.
- In scholastic Latin sources, the term came to denote the rational study of the doctrines of the Christian religion, or (more precisely) the academic discipline which investigated the coherence and implications of the language and claims of the Bible and of the theological tradition (the latter often as represented in Peter Lombard's *Sentences*, a book of extracts from the Church Fathers).
- It is the last of these senses (theology as the rational study of the teachings of a religion or of several religions) that lies behind most modern uses (though the second - theology as a discussion specifically of a religion's or several religions' teachings about God - is also found in some academic and ecclesiastical contexts; see the article on Theology Proper).
- 'Theology' can also now be used in a derived sense to mean 'a system of theoretical principles; an (impractical or rigid) ideology'

In academic theological circles, there is some debate as to whether theology is an activity peculiar to the Christian religion, such that the word 'theology' should be reserved for Christian theology, and other words used to name analogous discourses within other religious traditions. It is seen by some to be a term only appropriate to the study of religions that worship a deity (a *theos*), and to presuppose belief in the ability to speak and reason about this deity (in *logia*) - and so to be less appropriate in religious contexts which are organized differently (i.e. religions without a deity, or which deny that such subjects can be studied logically). (Hierology has been proposed as an alternative, more generic term.)

Analogous discourses

- Some academic inquiries within Buddhism, dedicated to the rational investigation of a Buddhist understanding of the world, prefer the designation Buddhist philosophy to the term Buddhist theology, since Buddhism lacks the same conception of a *theos*. Jose Ignacio Cabezon, who argues that the use of 'theology' *is* appropriate, can only do so, he says, because 'I take theology not to be restricted to discourse on God ... I take "theology" not to be restricted to its etymological meaning. In that latter sense, Buddhism is of course *a*theological, rejecting as it does the notion of God.'
- There is, within Hindu philosophy, a solid and ancient tradition of philosophical speculation on the nature of the universe, of God (termed Brahman in some schools of Hindu thought) and of the Atman (soul). The Sanskrit word for the various schools of Hindu philosophy is Darshana (meaning, view or viewpoint). Vaishnava theology has been a subject of study for many devotees, philosophers and scholars in India for centuries, has in recent decades also been taken on by a

number of academic institutions in Europe, such as the Oxford Centre for Hindu Studies and Bhaktivedanta College.

- In Islam, theological discussion which parallels Christian theological discussion has been a minor and even slightly disreputable activity, named "Kalam"; the Islamic analogue of Christian theological discussion would more properly be the investigation and elaboration of Islamic law, or "Fiqh". 'Kalam ... does not hold the leading place in Muslim thought that theology does in Christianity. To find an equivalent for "theology" in the Christian sense it is necessary to have recourse to several disciplines, and to the usul al-fiqh as much as to kalam.' (L. Gardet)
- In Judaism the historical absence of political authority has meant that most theological reflection has happened within the context of the Jewish community and synagogue, rather than within specialised academic institutions. Nevertheless Jewish theology has been historically very active and highly significant for Christian and Islamic Theology. Once again, however, the Jewish analogue of Christian theological discussion would more properly be Rabbinical discussion of Jewish law and Jewish Biblical commentaries.

Theology and the Academy

Theology has a significantly problematic position within Academia that is not shared by any other subject. Most universities founded before the modern era grew out of the church schools and monastic institutions of Western Europe during the High Middle Ages (e.g. University of Bologna,

Paris University and Oxford University). They were founded to train young men to serve the church in Theology and Law (often Church or Canon law). At such Universities Theological study was incomplete without Theological practice, including preaching, prayer and celebration of the Mass. Ancient Universities still maintain some of these links (e.g. having Chapels and Chaplains) and are more likely to teach Theology than other institutions.

During the High Middle Ages theology was therefore the ultimate subject at universities, being named "The Queen of the Sciences", and serving as the capstone to the Trivium and Quadrivium that young men were expected to study. This meant that the other subjects (including Philosophy) existed primarily to help with theological thought.

With the Enlightenment, universities began to change, teaching a wide range of subjects, especially in Germany, and from a Humanistic perspective. Theology was no longer the principal subject and Universities existed for many purposes, not only to train Clergy for established churches. Theology thus became unusual as the only subject to maintain a confessional basis in otherwise secular establishments.

As a result theology is often distinguished from many other established Academic disciplines that cover the same subject area. Those who contend it is different sometimes claim that it is distinguished by viewpoint (suggesting that theology is studied from within a faith, rather than from without) and by practical involvement (suggesting theology cannot be truly studied or understood without a practical faith - an idea that would have been familiar to some of the early Christian Church Fathers, who described the theologian as a person who "truly prays."). Others would claim that theology involves taking seriously claims internal to a religious tradition on their own terms, as topics for investigation and analysis - studying people's beliefs about God, rather than necessarily studying God, perhaps - even if that inquiry is not carried out by one who is committed to the relevant tradition, or involved in practice flowing from it.

Nevertheless theology should be distinguished from the following disciplines;

(a) Comparative religion/Religious studies
(b) Philosophy of religion
(c) The History of religions
(d) Psychology of religion
(e) Sociology of religion

All of these normally involve studying the historical or contemporary practices or ideas of one or several religious traditions using intellectual tools and frameworks which are not themselves specifically tied to any religious tradition, but are (normally) understood to be neutral or secular.

Even when it is distinguished from these other disciplines, however, some hold that the very idea of an academic discipline called 'theology', housed in institutions like Universities, is an inherently secular, Western notion. Noting that 'reasoned discourse about religion/God' is an idea with a very particular intellectual pedigree, with at least some roots in Graeco-Roman intellectual culture, they argue that this idea actually brings with it deep assumptions which we can now see to be related to ideas underlying 'secularism': i.e., the whole idea of reasoned discourse about God/religion suggests the possibility of a common intellectual framework or set of tools for investigating, comparing and evaluating traditions - an idea with a strong affinity for a 'secular' worldview in which religions are seen as particular choices, set within an overarching religiously neutral public sphere. They argue that even those who pursue this discourse as a way of deepening their commitment to and expertise in their own tradition, perhaps even so as to become promoters and propagators of it, often do so in a way which underlines this same 'secular' atmosphere - by assuming the communicability of their religious views (as explored and explained by theological discourse) within a neutral intellectual market-place.

In Europe, the traditional places for the study of theology have been universities and seminaries. Typically the Protestant state churches have trained their ministers in universities while the Roman Catholic church has used seminaries as well as universities for both the clergy and the laity. However, the secularization of European states has closed down the theological faculties in many countries while the Catholic church has increased the academical level of its priests by founding a number of pontifical universities.

In some countries, some state-funded Universities have theology Departments (sometimes, but not always, Universities with a medieval or early-modern pedigree), which can have a variety of formal relationships to Christian churches, or to institutions within other religious traditions. These range from Departments of Theology which have only informal or ad-hoc links to religious institutions to countries like Finland and Sweden, which have state universities with faculties of theology training Lutheran priests as well as teachers and scholars of religion - although students from the latter faculties can also go on to typical graduate careers such as marketing, business or administration, even if this is frowned upon by some.

In the United States, the Supreme Court ruled that the United States Constitution prevents the study of theology from enjoying state endorsement. Theological studies (sometimes called Biblical studies) take place in a large number of private universities and seminaries, at varying academic levels, and with various different degrees of academic freedom. Some hold that many of these American contexts for the study of theology have less academic freedom than the faculties of theology in many European state universities, pointing out that, at least in some of these contexts, theologians who end up with views deemed "heretical" by the denomination upholding the institution and may find themselves out of work. On the other hand, there are those who claim that the "openness" of the European faculties of theology is really an openness towards liberal or modernist theological trends, and that those who hold more conservative theological views have very little of practical freedom.

III

THEOLOGICAL ANTHROPOLOGY

Theological anthropology is the branch of theology which is concerned with the study of humankind, or anthropology, in relation to the divine. In a theological context, it is usually referred to simply as anthropology.

Christian Anthropology

> Christianlly could be condensed into four words: Admit, submit, commit, and transmit's"
>
> —*William Wilberforce*

In the context of Christian theology, theological anthropology refers to the study of the human ("anthropology") as it relates to God. It differs from the social science of anthropology, which primarily deals with the comparative study of the physical and social characteristics of humanity across times and places.

One aspect studies the innate nature or constitution of the human, known as the nature of humankind (known as the nature of man before the popularity of gender-neutral language). It is concerned with the relationship between notions such as body, soul and spirit which together form a person, based on their descriptions in the Bible. There are three traditional views of the human constitution – trichotomism, dichotomism and monism (in the sense of anthropology).

Body

The body is the corporeal or physical aspect of a human being. Christians have traditionally believed that the body will be resurrected at the end of the age.

Rudolf Bultmann states the following:

> "That *soma* belongs inseparably, constitutively, to human existence is most clearly evident from the fact that Paul cannot conceive even of a future human existence after death, 'when that which is perfect is come' as an existence without *soma* – in contrast to the view of those in Corinth who deny the resurrection (1 Cor. 15, especially vv. 35ff.)."
>
> "Man does not have a *soma*; he is a *soma*"

Soul

The semantic domain of Biblical soul is based on the Hebrew word *nepes* which presumably means "breath" or "breathing being". This word never means an immortal soul or an incorporeal part of the human being that can survive death of the body as the spirit of dead. This word usually designates the person as a whole or its physical life. In the Septuagint *nepes* is mostly translated as *psyche* (øõ÷Þ) and, exceptionally, in the Book of Joshua as *empneon* that is "breathing being".

The New Testament follows the terminology of the Septuagint, and thus uses the word *psyche* with the Hebrew semantic domain and not the Greek, that is an invisible power (or ever more, for Platonists, immortal and immaterial) that gives life and motion to the body and is responsible for its attributes.

In Patristic thought, towards the end of the 2nd century *psyche* was understood in more a Greek than a Hebrew way, and it was contrasted with the body. In the 3rd century, with the influence of Origen, there was the establishing of the doctrine of the inherent immortality of the soul and its divine nature. Origen also taught the transmigration of the souls and their preexistence, but these views were officially rejected in 553 in the Fifth Ecumenical Council. Inherent immortality of the soul was accepted among western and eastern theologians throughout the middle ages, and after the Reformation, as evidenced by the Westminster Confession.

On the other hand, a number of modern Protestant scholars have adopted views similar to conditional immortality, including Edward Fudge and Clark Pinnock; however the majority of adherents hold the traditional doctrine. In the last six decades, conditional immortality, or better "immortality by grace" of the soul has also been widely accepted among Eastern Orthodox theologians, by returning to the views of the late 2nd century, where immortality was still considered as a gift granted with the value of Jesus' death and resurrection.

Spirit

The spirit (Hebrew *ruach*, Greek *pneuma*, which can also mean "breath") is likewise an immaterial component. It is often used interchangeably with "soul", although trichotomists believe that the spirit is distinct from the soul.

"When Paul speaks of the *pneuma* of man he does not mean some higher principle within him or some special intellectual or spiritual faculty of his, but simply his self, and the only questions is whether the self is regarded in some particular aspect when it is called *pneuma*. In the first place, it apparently is regarded in the same way as when it is called *psyche* – viz. as the self that lives in man's attitude, in the orientation of his will."

Flesh

"Flesh" is usually considered synonymous with "body", referring to the corporeal aspect of a human being. The apostle Paul contrasts flesh and spirit in Romans 7-8.

Constitution or Nature of the Person

Historically, Christian theologians have differed on how many components make up the human being.

Two parts (Dichotomism)

The traditional Christian view, still held by a large number of lay Christians and theologians, is that the human being is made up of 2 components: material (body/flesh) and spiritual (soul/spirit). The soul or spirit departs from the body at death, and will be reunited with the body at the resurrection.

Three parts (Trichotomism)

A minority of theologians have argued that human beings are made up of three distinct components: body/flesh, soul, and spirit. This is technically known as trichotomism. The biblical texts typically used to support this position are 1 Thessalonians 5:23 and Hebrews 4:12.

One part (Monism)

Modern theologians increasingly hold to the view that the human being is an indissoluble unity. This is known as holism or monism. The body and soul are not considered separate components of a person, but rather as two facets of a united whole. It is argued that this more accurately represents Hebrew thought, whereas body-soul dualism is more characteristic of Greek philosophy and Platonic thought. Monism also appears to be more consistent with modern neuroscience, which has revealed that the so-called "higher functions" of the mind are emergent from the brain, rather than being based in an immaterial soul as was previously thought.

An influential exponent of this view was liberal theologian Rudolf Bultmann. Oscar Cullmann was influential in popularizing it.

Origin of Humanity

The Bible teaches in the book of Genesis the humans were created by God. Some Christians believe that this must have involved a miraculous creative act, while others are comfortable with the idea that God worked through the evolutionary process.

God's image in the human

The book of Genesis also teaches that human beings, male and female, were created in the image of God. The exact meaning of this has been debated throughout church history.

Origin/transmission of the soul

There are two opposing views about how the soul originates in each human being. *Creationism* teaches that God creates a "fresh" soul within each human embryo at or some time shortly after conception. The Roman Catholic Church officially teaches the creationist position. Notably, this is not to be confused with creationism as a view of the origins of life and the universe.

Traducianism, by contrast, teaches that the soul is inherited from the individual's parents, along with his or her biological material.

Sinful Nature

Christian theology traditionally teaches the corruption of human nature. However, there have been a range of views held throughout church history. Pelagius taught that human nature is not so corrupt that we cannot overcome sin. Arminians believe that our nature is corrupt, but that free will can still operate. Saint Augustine believed that all humans are born into the sin and guilt of Adam, and are powerless to do good without grace. John Calvin developed the doctrine of total depravity.

Death and Afterlife

Christian anthropology has implications for beliefs about death and the afterlife. The Christian church has traditionally taught that the soul of each individual separates from the body at death, to be reunited at the resurrection. This is closely related to the doctrine of the immortality of the soul. For example, the Westminster Confession (chapter XXXII) states:

"The bodies of men, after death, return to dust, and see corruption: but their souls, which neither die nor sleep, having an immortal subsistence, immediately return to God who gave them"

Intermediate state

The question then arises: where exactly does the disembodied soul "go" at death? Theologians refer to this subject as the intermediate state. The Old Testament speaks of a place called *sheol* where the spirits of the dead reside. In the New Testament, *hades*, the classical Greek realm of the dead, takes the place of *sheol*. In particular, Jesus teaches in Luke 16:19-31 (Lazarus and Dives) that *hades* consists of two separate "sections", one for the righteous and one for the unrighteous. His teaching is consistent with intertestamental Jewish thought on the subject.

Fully developed Christian theology goes a step further; on the basis of such texts as Luke 23:43 and Philippians 1:23, it has traditionally been taught that the souls of the dead are received immediately either into heaven or hell, where they will experience a foretaste of their eternal destiny prior to the resurrection. (Roman Catholicism teaches a third possible location, Purgatory, though this is denied by Protestants.)

"the souls of the righteous, being then made perfect in holiness, are received into the highest heavens, where they behold the face of God, in light and glory, waiting for the full redemption of their bodies. And the souls of the wicked are cast into hell, where they remain in torments and utter darkness, reserved to the judgment of the great day." (*Westminster Confession*)

Some Christian groups which stress a monistic anthropology deny that the soul can exist consciously apart from the body. For example, the Seventh-day Adventist church teaches that the intermediate state is an unconscious sleep; this teaching is informally known as "soul sleep".

Final state

In Christian belief, both the righteous and the unrighteous will be resurrected at the last judgment. The righteous will receive incorruptible, immortal bodies (1 Corinthians 15), while the unrighteous will be sent to hell. Traditionally, Christians have believed that hell will be a place of eternal physical and psychological punishment. In the last 2 centuries, annihilationism has become more popular.

4

SOCIAL ANTHROPOLOGY

Social anthropology is the branch of anthropology that studies how currently living human beings behave in social groups. Basically, practitioners of social anthropology investigate, often through long term, intensive field studies (including participant observation methods), the social organization of a particular people: customs, economic and political organization, law and conflict resolution, patterns of consumption and exchange, kinship and family structure, gender relations, childrearing and socialization, religion, and so on.

Further social anthropology also explores the role of meanings, ambiguities and contradictions of social life, patterns of sociality, violence and conflict, and the underlying logics of social behaviour. Social anthropologists are particularly skilled in the interpretation of narrative, ritual and symbolic behaviour not merely as 'text,' but with communication examined in relation to action, practice, and the historical context in which it is embedded. Social anthropologists address the diversity of positions and perspectives to be found within any social group.

It is pertinent to note that the subject has both ethical and reflexive dimensions. It has developed an awareness of the sense in which scholars create their objects of study and the ways in which anthropologists themselves may contribute to processes of change in the societies they study.

Social anthropology is distinguished from subjects such as economics or political science by its holistic range and the attention it gives to the diversity of culture and society across the world, and the capacity this gives the discipline to re-examine Euro-American assumptions. It is differentiated from sociology both in its main methods (based on long-term participant observation and linguistic competence), its commitment to the relevance and illumination provided by micro studies, and its extension beyond strictly social phenomena to culture, art, individuality, and cognition. While some social anthropologists use quantitative methods (particularly those whose research touches on topics such as local economies, demography, or health and illness), social anthropologists generally emphasize qualitative analysis of long-term fieldwork, rather than the more quantitative methods used by most economists or sociologists.

Specialisations within social anthropology shift as its objects of study are transformed and as new intellectual paradigms appear; ethnomusicology and medical anthropology afford examples of current, well-defined specialisms. Ethnomusicology studies world musics, relating sounds, practices and ideas to their broader social and cultural contexts. Through fieldwork and participant observation as well as musical analysis, it investigates styles and genres, composition and performance, to illuminate issues of aesthetics, gender, power, meaning and social organisation.

Medical anthropology is concerned with experiences of health, illness and trauma in different social and cultural settings as with, for example, AIDS transmission in Africa, and India or the consequences of war and ethnic conflict. Its comparative perspectives are increasingly relevant as relationships between western and other healing systems change, while new areas of the subject emerge as drug and technologically-based care impacts upon culturally specific notions of body, health, illness and ageing, generating new ethical dilemmas.

Further more recent and currently emergent areas within social anthropology include: the relation between cultural diversity and new findings in cognitive development; social and ethical understandings of novel technologies; emergent forms of 'the family' and other new socialities modelled on kinship; the ongoing social fall-out of the demise of state socialism; the politics of resurgent religiosity; analysis of audit cultures and accountability. The subject has been enlivened by, and has contributed to, approaches from other disciplines, such as philosophy (e.g ethics, phenomenology, logic), the history of science, psychoanalysis, and social linguistics.

It is significant to note that social anthropology has historical roots in a number of 19th-century disciplines, including ethnology, folklore studies, and Classics, among others. Its immediate precursor took shape in the work of Edward Burnett Tylor and James George Frazer in the late 19th century and underwent major changes in both method and theory during the period 1890-1920 with a new emphasis on original fieldwork, long-term holistic study of social behavior in natural settings, and the introduction of French and German social theory.

In fact modern social anthropology was founded in Great Britain following World War I through a methodological revolution pioneered by Bronislaw Malinowski's meticulous process-oriented fieldwork in the Trobriand Islands of Melanesia between 1915 and 1918 and through Alfred Radcliffe-Brown's theoretical program for systematic comparison that was based on a conception of rigorous fieldwork and the structure-functionalist conception of Durkheim's sociology. Other intellectual founders include W. H. R. Rivers and A. C. Haddon, whose orientation reflected the contemprorary Volkerpsychologie of Wilhelm Wundt and Adolf Bastian, and Sir E. B. Tylor, who defined anthropology as a positivistic science following Auguste Comte. Edmund Leach (1962) defined social anthropology as a kind of comparative micro-sociology based on intensive fieldwork studies. There was never a settled theoretical orthodoxy on the nature of science and society but always a tension between several views that were seriously opposed.

In the aftermath of World War II, sociocultural anthropology as comprised by the fields of ethnography and ethnology diverged into an American school of cultural anthropology while social anthropology diversified in Europe by challenging the principles of structure-functionalism, absorbing ideas from Claude Levi-Strauss's structuralism and from Max Gluckman's Manchester school, and embracing the study of conflict, change, urban anthropology, and networks.

A remarkable development is the foundation of European Association of Social Anthropologists was founded in 1989 as a society of scholarship at a meeting of founder members from fourteen European countries, supported by the Wenner-Gren Foundation for Anthropological Research. The Association seeks to advance anthropology in Europe by organizing biennial conferences and by editing its academic journal, Social Anthropology/Anthropologie Sociale.

Other universities outside Britain do have departments of Social Anthropology, including in the United States (e.g., Stanford University, Harvard University, University of Chicago) and many non-European anthropologists identify themselves as social anthropologists, and often in ways not anticipated by the founders of the field, as for example in the subfield of structure and dynamics.

Anthropologists associated with British Social Anthropology

- Bronislaw Malinowski
- Alfred Radcliffe-Brown
- Mary Douglas
- E. E. Evans-Pritchard
- Rosemary Firth
- Raymond Firth
- Meyer Fortes
- Ernest Gellner
- Adam Kuper
- Edmund Leach
- Alan Macfarlane
- David Maybury-Lewis
- Siegfried Frederick Nadel
- Murray Leaf
- Marilyn Strathern
- James Woodburn
- Andre Beteille

- Audrey Richards
- Victor Turner

II

NOMADS

Nomadic people, also known as nomads, are communities of people that move from place to place in the deserts or winter-climated places, rather than settling down in one location. People who move from place to place who are not in the desert or winter areas are called gypsies. Many cultures have been traditionally nomadic, but traditional nomadic behavior is increasingly rare in industrialized countries. There are three kinds of nomads, hunter-gatherers, pastoral nomads, and peripatetic nomads. Nomadic hunter-gatherers have by far the longest-lived subsistence method in human history, following seasonally available wild plants and game. Pastoralists raise herds and move with them so as not to deplete pasture beyond recovery in any one area. Peripatetic nomads are more common in industrialized nations traveling from place to place offering a trade wherever they go.

For more than one million years before domestication, nomadic hunter-gatherers (also known as foragers) moved from campsite to campsite following game and wild fruits and vegetables.

She following communicaties include the major hunter-gathered nomadic groups:

- Various groups of Pygmies, such as the Mbuti of the Ituri Rainforest in the Democratic Republic of the Congo
- The Bushmen (also known as Basarwa or San)

of southern Africa

- Some Native Americans prior to Western contact
- Most Indigenous Australians prior to Western contact
- The Negritos of Southeast Asia
- Some Adivasi tribal people of India

Pastoral Nomads

"Nomad" is often shorthand for "pastoral nomad," which refers to one whose subsistence is based upon domestication of animals. This nomadic pastoralism is thought to have developed in three stages that accompanied population growth and an increase in the complexity of social organization. Karim Sadr has proposed the following stages:

- Pastoralism: This is a mixed economy with a symbiosis within the family.
- Agropastoralism: This is when symbiosis is between segments or clans within an ethnic group.
- True Nomadism: This is when symbiosis is at the regional level, generally between specialized nomadic and agricultural populations.

Nomadic pastoralism seems to have developed as a part of the secondary products revolution proposed by Andrew Sherratt, in which early pre-pottery Neolithic cultures that had used animals as live meat ("on the hoof") began also using animals for their secondary products, for example, milk and its associated dairy products, wool and other animal hair, hides and consequently leather, manure for fuel and fertilizer, and traction.

The first nomadic pastoral society developed in the period from 8500-6500 BC in the area of the southern

Levant. There, during a period of increasing aridity, PPNB cultures in the Sinai were replaced by a nomadic, pastoral pottery-using culture, which seems to have been a cultural fusion between a newly arrived Mesolithic people from Egypt (the Harifian culture), adopting their nomadic hunting lifestyle to the raising of stock. This lifestyle quickly developed into what Jaris Yurins has called the circum-Arabian nomadic pastoral techno-complex and is possibly associated with the appearance of Semitic languages in the region of the Ancient Near East. The rapid spread of such nomadic pastoralism was typical of such later developments as of the Yamnaya culture of the horse and cattle nomads of the Eurasian steppe, or of the Turko-Mongol spread of the later Middle Ages.

Some Praminents pastoral nomads

- Ababdeh
- Bedouin Arabs
- Cumans
- Crimean Tatars (certain groups)
- Dzungars
- Eurasian Avars
- Finns
- Fulanis
- Himba
- Huns
- Indo-Aryans (certain groups)
    - Gujars
    - Mitanni
    - Dhangars

  - Rajputs
  - Rigvedic tribes
  - Roma (Gypsies)
- Iranians (certain groups)
  - Alans
  - Dahae
  - Bakhtiari of Iran
  - Hephthalites
  - Hunas
  - Kuchis (Kochai)
  - Parni
  - Parthians
  - Sarmatians
  - Scythians
- Kalmyks
- Kazakhs
- Khazars
- Kurumbar
- Magyars
- Moken
- Mongols
- Moors
- Mrazig of Tunisia
- Nenetses
- Nogais
- Nuer
- Pechenegs

- Somalis (certain clans)
- Tibetans
- Toubou
- Tuaregs
- Turks
- Turkmens
- Trekboers
- Wu Hu
- Yörük
- Some reindeer-herding Sami communities
- Roma (Gypsies)
  - Kalderash
  - Gitano (AKA Cale)
  - Manush (AKA Sinti)
  - Romnichal
- Irish Travellers
- Some Saami communities

One of the consequences of the break-up of the Soviet Union and the subsequent political independence and economic collapse of its Central Asian republics is the resurgence of pastoral nomadism. Taking the Kyrgyz people as a representative example, nomadism was the center of their economy prior to Russian colonization at the turn of the C19/C20, when they were settled into agricultural villages. The population became increasingly urbanized after World War II, but some people continued to take their herds of horses and cows to the high pasture (*jailoo*) every summer, i.e. a pattern of transhumance. Since the 1990s, as the cash economy shrunk, unemployed relatives were absorbed back on the family farm, and the importance of this form of nomadism has increased. The symbols of nomadism, specifically the crown of the grey felt tent known as the yurt, appears on the national flag, emphasizing the centrality of their nomadic history and past in the creation of the modern nation of Kyrgyzstan.

QUESTION FOR PRACTICE

1. What is distinctive about the aims and activities of social anthropologists?.
2. Contrast the main features of pastoral societies with those of hunter-gatherers.
3. As somebody from a society which is state-organised what do you notice about societies with no formal government and no classes? Discuss.
4. Exchange involves negative as well as positive, vengeance as well as doing people favours. Discuss.
5. Are you convinced by writers who claim that witchcraft accusations can be socially constructive?
6. Cargo cults look stupid and irrational to a casual visitor in their area, but are basically sensible and well conceived. Assess this claim.
7. What are the main features of the social roles of kings?
8. How useful do you find the distinction between domestic and public domains when you are seeking to explain gender differentiation?
9. In which respects may ethnographic films be

said to 'challenge' conventional written representations in anthropology?

10. What contribution can anthropologist make to the study of biomedicine?
11. Ethnicity is a response to contemporary circumstances, not a resurgence of traditionalism. Discuss.
12. Should the term 'peasant' be rejected for reasons of 'political correctness'?
13. Why is it inadequate to address the problems of poor people in terms solely of improving their productive technologies.
14. Is mafia a specialist form of patronage?
15. To what extent have the 'egalitarian' ideologies of tradition in African states influenced the development of modern Islamic republics?
16. Describe and discuss the key structural features of ONE swiddening society.
17. In the simplest societies gender is not an issue. Discuss.
18. Why is marriage so important as a social institution?
19. Examine the implications of seasonal mobility in the social organisation of any ONE pastoral society.
20. Gifts are never freely given. Discuss with reference to the comparative anthropology of exchange.
21. Critically consider how anthropologists have analysed blood-feud as a mechanism of social control in stateless societies.

22. What can studies of EITHER witchcraft accusations OR cargo cults reveal about the relationship between underlying beliefs and social experience?
23. Describe any religious ritual with which you are familiar and discuss its significance for creating and affirming a sense of communal identity.
24. Compare and contrast the relationship between language and status in at least TWO societies.
25. Discuss the way in which kinship ties continue to be important in industrialised societies among the majority and/or minority populations of those countries.
26. Anthropologists should not act as consultants for mult-national companies operating 'the Third World'. Discuss.
27. How would you identify a group of people to be peasants?
28. Is there a realistic comparison between red revolutions and green revolutions, or is this usage just a play on words?
29. Modern consumption leads to the elimination of cultural differences. Discuss.
30. Notions of the causality of illness underpin the distinction between culturally specific medical systems. Discuss.

5

CULTURAL ANTHROPOLOGY

> "Culture is not just an ornament; it is the expansion of a nations character and at the same time it is a powerful instrument to mould character. The end of culture is right living."
>
> —*W. Somerset Maugham*

Cultural anthropology is one of four fields of anthropology (the holistic study of humanity) as it developed in the United States. It is the branch of anthropology that has developed and promoted "culture" as a meaningful scientific concept; it is also the branch of anthropology that studies cultural variation among humans.

Basically the anthropological concept of "culture" reflects in part a reaction against earlier Western discourses based on an opposition between "culture" and "nature", according to which some human beings lived in a "state of nature". Anthropologists argue that culture *is* "human nature," and that all people have a capacity to classify experiences, encode classifications symbolically, and teach such abstractions to others. Since humans acquire culture through learning (the processes of enculturation and socialization), people living in different places or different circumstances may develop different cultures. Anthropologists have also pointed out that through culture people can adapt to their environment in non-genetic ways, so people living in different environments will often have different cultures. Much of anthropological theory has originated in an appreciation of and interest in the tension between the local (particular cultures) and the global (a universal human nature, or the web of connections between people in distinct places/ circumstances).

It is pertinent here to note that parallel with the rise of cultural anthropology in the United States, social anthropology, in which "sociality" is the central concept and which focuses on the study of social statuses and roles, groups, institutions, and the relations among them, developed as an academic discipline in Great Britain. Some anthropologists have drawn on both traditions and identify themselves as socio-cultural anthropologists.

Modern cultural anthropology has its origins in, and developed in reaction to, 19th century "ethnology", which involves the organized comparison of human societies. Scholars like E.B. Tylor and J.G. Frazer in England worked mostly with materials collected by others – usually missionaries, explorers, or colonial officials – this earned them their current sobriquet of "arm-chair anthropologists".

Ethnologists had an especial interest in why people living in different parts of the world sometimes had similar beliefs and practices. In addressing this question, ethnologists in the 19th century divided into two schools of thought. Some, like Grafton Elliot Smith, argued that different groups must somehow have learned from one another, however indirectly; in other words, they argued that cultural traits spread from one place to another, or "diffused". Other ethnologists argued that different groups had the capability of inventing similar beliefs and practices independently. Some of those who advocated "independent invention", like Lewis Henry Morgan, additionally supposed that similarities meant that different groups had passed through the same stages of cultural evolution.

In fact most of the 20th century anthropologists largely reject the notion that all human societies must pass through the same stages in the same order. Some 20th century ethnologists, like Julian Steward, have instead argued that such similarities reflected similar adaptations to similar environments. Others, like Claude Lévi-Strauss (who was influenced both by American cultural anthropology and by French Durkheimian sociology), have argued that apparent patterns of development reflect fundamental similarities in the structure of human thought.

As an important development in the 20th century most cultural (and social) anthropologists turned to the study of ethnography, in which an anthropologist actually lives among another society for a considerable period of time, simultaneously participating in and observing the social and cultural life of the group. Bronislaw Malinowski (who conducted fieldwork in the Trobriand Islands and taught in England) developed this method, and Franz Boas (who conducted fieldwork in Baffin Island and taught in the United States) promoted it. Boas's students drew on his conception of culture and cultural relativism to develop cultural anthropology in the United States. Simultaneously, Malinowski and A.R. Radcliffe Brown´s students were developing social anthropology in the Great Britian. Whereas cultural anthropology focused on symbols and values, social anthropology focused on social groups and institutions.

Today socio-cultural anthropologists attend to all these elements completly.

No doubt 19th century ethnologists saw "diffusion" and "independent invention" as mutually exclusive and competing theories, most ethnographers quickly reached a consensus that both processes occur, and that both can plausibly account for cross-cultural similarities. But these ethnographers pointed out the superficiality of many such similarities, and that even traits that spread through diffusion often changed their meaning and functions as they moved from one society to another. Accordingly, these anthropologists showed less interest in comparing cultures, generalizing about human nature, or discovering universal laws of cultural development, than in understanding particular cultures in those cultures' own terms.

Such ethnographers and their students promoted the idea of "cultural relativism", the view that one can only understand another person's beliefs and behaviors in the context of the culture in which he or she lived.

Remarkably, in the early 20th century socio-cultural anthropology developed in different forms in Europe and in the United States. European "social anthropologists" focused on observed social behaviors and on "social structure", that is, on relationships among social roles (e.g. husband and wife, or parent and child) and social institutions (e.g. religion, economy, and politics). American "cultural anthropologists" focused on the ways people expressed their view of themselves and their world, especially in symbolic forms (such as art and myths).

These two approaches frequently converged (kinship, for example, and leadership function both as symbolic systems and as social institutions), and generally complemented one another. As of now, almost all socio-cultural anthropologists refer to the work of both sets of predecessors, and have an equal interest in what people do and in what people say.

Contemporary Developments

Currently ethnography continues to dominate socio-cultural anthropology. Nevertheless, many contemporary socio-cultural anthropologists have rejected earlier models of ethnography which they claim treated local cultures as bounded and isolated. These anthropologists continue to concern themselves with the distinct ways people in different locales experience and understand their lives, but they often argue that one cannot understand these particular ways of life solely in the local context; one must analyze them (they say) in the context of regional or even global political and economic relations. Notable proponents of this approach include Arjun Appadurai, James Clifford, George Marcus, Sidney Mintz, Michael Taussig and Eric Wolf.

A growing trend in anthropological research and analysis is the use of multi-sited ethnography, discussed in George Marcus's article "Ethnography In/Of the World System: the Emergence of Multi-Sited Ethnography". Looking at culture as embedded in macro-constructions of a global social order, multi-sited ethnography uses traditional methodology in various locations both spatially and temporally. Through this methodology greater insight can be gained when examining the impact of world-systems on local and global communities.

Also emerging in multi-sited ethnography are greater interdisciplinary approaches to fieldwork, bringing in methods from cultural studies, media studies, science and technology studies, and others. In multi-sited ethnography research tracks a subject across spatial and temporal boundaries. For example, a multi-sited ethnography may follow a "thing," such as a particular commodity, as it transfers through the networks of global capitalism.

Multi-sited ethnography may also follow ethnic groups in diaspora, stories or rumours that appear in multiple locations and in multiple time periods, metaphors that appear in multiple ethnographic locations, or the biographies of individual people or groups as they move through space and time. It may also follow conflicts that transcend boundaries. Multi-sited ethnographies, such as Nancy Scheper-Hughes's ethnography of the international black market for the trade of human organs. In this research she follows organs as they transfer through various legal and illegal networks of capitalism, as well as the rumours and urban legends that circulate in impoverished communities about child kidnapping and organ theft.

Of late, it is being observed that, sociocultural anthropologists have increasingly turned their investigative eye on to "Western" culture. For example, Philippe Bourgois won the Margaret Mead Award in 1997 for *In Search of Respect*, a study of the entrepreneurs in a Harlem crack-den. Also growing more popular are ethnographies of professional communities, such as laboratory researchers, Wall Street investors, law firms, or IT computer employees etc.

It is most interesting to note that the title a college gives its introductory anthropology course can be used as a measure of that department's anthropological focus. Some departments are inspired by the branching developments in social anthropology, often with a British or European influence, and may title an introductory course accordingly. Departments influenced by American thinking, which takes a more holistic approach, frequently title their introductory course "cultural anthropology" instead of anthropology.

Media Anthropology

Anthropology of media (also anthropology of mass media, media anthropology) is an area of study within social or cultural anthropology that emphasizes ethnographic studies as a means of understanding producers, audiences, and other cultural and social aspects of mass media.

What is distinctive about anthropology of media is the use of ethnography. Within media studies, media ethnographies have been of increasing interest. However these have often not followed anthropological approaches to ethnography like participant observation and long term fieldwork. These differences mean that anthropologists who take an interest in the media see themselves as a subfield distinct from ethnographic approaches in media studies and cultural studies.

The anthropology of media is a fairly inter-disciplinary area, with a wide range of other influences. The theories used in the anthropology of media range from practice approaches, attributable to theorists such as Pierre Bourdieu, as well as discussions of the appropriation and adaptation of new technologies and practices. Theoretical approaches have also been picked up from visual anthropology and from film theory as well as from studies of ritual and performance studies (e.g. dance and theatre). Theoretical discussions have also been picked up from studies of consumption, audience reception in media studies, new media and network theories, theories of globalisation, theories of international civil society, and discussions of participatory communications, and governance from development studies.

Ethnographic contexts

The types of ethnographic contexts explored in the anthropology of media range from the production of media: ethnographies of newsrooms in newspapers, journalists in the field, film production and so on, as well as reception studies, following audiences in their responses to media. Other types include cyber anthropology - a relatively new area of internet research, as well as ethnographies of other contexts which happen to include media, such as development work, social movements, health education. This is in addition to many classic ethnographic contexts, where media such as radio, the press, new media and television have started to make their presences felt.

II

FOLKLORE

In conventional sense, folklore is the body of expressive culture, including tales, music, dance, legends, oral history, proverbs, jokes, popular beliefs, customs, and so forth within a particular population comprising the traditions (including oral traditions) of that culture, subculture, or group. It is also the set of practices through which those expressive genres are shared. The academic and usually ethnographic study of folklore is sometimes called folkloristics.

In the true sense, the concept of folklore developed as part of the 19th century ideology of romantic nationalism, leading to the reshaping of oral traditions to serve modern ideological goals; only in the 20th century did ethnographers begin to attempt to record folklore without overt political goals. The Brothers Grimm, Wilhelm and Jakob Grimm, collected orally transmitted German tales and published the first series as *Kinder- und Hausmärchen* ("Children's and Household Tales") in 1812.

Remarkably, for the first time the term was coined in 1846 by an Englishman, William Thoms, who wanted to use an Anglo-Saxon term for what was then called "popular antiquities." Johann Gottfried von Herder first advocated the deliberate recording and preservation of folklore to document the authentic spirit, tradition, and identity of the German people; the belief that there can be such authenticity is one of the tenets of the romantic nationalism which Herder developed. The definition most widely accepted by current scholars of the field is "artistic communication in small groups," coined by Dan Ben-Amos a scholar at the University of Pennsylvania, and the term, and the associated field of study, now include non-verbal art forms and customary practices.

While folklore can contain religious or mythic elements, it equally concerns itself with the sometimes mundane traditions of everyday life. Folklore frequently ties the practical and the esoteric into one narrative package. It has often been conflated with mythology, and vice versa, because it has been assumed that any figurative story that does not pertain to the dominant beliefs of the time is not of the same status as those dominant beliefs. Thus, Roman religion is called "myth" by Christians. In that way, both myth and folklore have become catch-all terms for all figurative narratives which do not correspond with the dominant belief structure. Sometimes "folklore" is religious in nature, like the tales of the Welsh *Mabinogion* or those found in Icelandic skaldic poetry. Many of the tales in the

Golden Legend of Jacob de Voragine also embody folklore elements in a Christian context: examples of such Christian mythology are the themes woven round Saint George or Saint Christopher. In this case, the term "folklore" is being used in a pejorative sense. That is, while the tales of Odin the Wanderer have a religious value to the Norse who composed the stories, because it does not fit into a Christian configuration it is not considered "religious" by Christians who may instead refer to it as "folklore."

Folk tales are general term for different varieties of traditional narrative. The telling of stories appears to be a cultural universal, common to basic and complex societies alike. Even the forms folktales take are certainly similar from culture to culture, and comparative studies of themes and narrative ways have been successful in showing these relationships. Also it is considered to be an oral tale to be told for everybody.

On the other hand, folklore can be used to accurately describe a figurative narrative, which has no sacred or religious content. In the Jungian view, which is but one method of analysis, it may instead pertain to unconscious psychological patterns, instincts or archetypes of the mind. This lore may or may not have components of the fantastic (such as magic, ethereal beings or the personification of inanimate objects). These folktales may or may not emerge from a religious tradition, but nevertheless speak to deep psychological issues. The familiar folklore, "Hansel and Gretel," is an example of this fine line. The manifest purpose of the tale may primarily be one of mundane instruction regarding forest safety or secondarily a cautionary tale about the dangers of famine to large families, but its latent meaning may evoke a strong emotional response due to the widely understood themes and motifs such as "The Terrible

Mother", "Death," and "Atonement with the Father." There can be both a moral and psychological scope to the work, as well as entertainment value, depending upon the nature of the teller, the style of the telling, the ages of the audience members, and the overall context of the performance. Folklorists generally resist universal interpretations of narratives and, wherever possible, analyze oral versions of tellings in specific contexts, rather than print sources, which often show the work or bias of the writer or editor.

Contemporary narratives common in the Western world include the urban legend. There are many forms of folklore that are so common, however, that most people do not realize they are folklore, such as riddles, children's rhymes and ghost stories, rumors (including conspiracy theories), gossip, ethnic stereotypes, and holiday customs and life-cycle rituals. UFO abduction narratives can be seen, in some sense, to refigure the tales of pre-Christian Europe, or even such tales in the Bible as the Ascent of Elijah to heaven. Adrienne Mayor, in introducing a bibliography on the topic, noted that most modern folklorists are largely unaware of classical parallels and precedents, in materials that are only partly represented by the familiar designation *Aesopica*: "Ancient Greek and Roman literature contains rich troves of folklore and popular beliefs, many of which have counterparts in modern contemporary legends".

6

PHYSICAL (BIOLOGICAL) ANTHROPOLOGY

Physical (Biological) Anthropology is a main branch of the anthropology. Here in this chapter we will give an overview of the discipline. Thereafter all major subfields (branches) of the physical anthropology will be highlighted to have a thorough glimpse of it.

Basically, Biological anthropology, or physical anthropology is a branch of anthropology that studies the mechanisms of biological evolution, genetic inheritance, human adaptability and variation, primatology, primate morphology, and the fossil record of human evolution.

Physical anthropology developed in the 19th century, prior to the rise of Alfred Russel Wallace's and Charles Darwin's theories of natural selection and Gregor Mendel's work on genetics. Physical anthropology was so called because all of its data was physical (fossils, especially human bones). With the rise of Darwinian theory and the modern synthesis, anthropologists had access to new forms of data, and many began to call themselves "biological anthropologists." But physical anthropology is widely popular.

Some of the early branches of physical anthropology, such as early anthropometry, are now rejected as pseudoscience. Metrics such as the cephalic index were used to derive behavioral characteristics. Two of the earliest founders of scientific physical anthropology were Paul Broca and Franz Boas.

Subfield of Study

The following are the main branches of physical Anthropology:

- Primatology, the study of primates,
- Population genetics, the study of biological human variability and diversity (related to evolutionary biology)
- Human adaptation, the study of human adaptive responses (physiological, developmental, and genetic) to environmental stress and variation.
- Human anatomy the study of the anatomy and physiology of humans and their ancestors.
- Human evolution including:
    - Paleoanthropology, the study of fossil evidence for human evolution.
    - Human behavioral ecology, the study of behavioral adaptations such as foraging, reproduction, and ontogeny from an evolutionary ecological perspective.
- Neuroanthropology, the study of the evolution of the human brain, and of culture as a neurological adaptation of the species to its environment.

The study of human evolution often involves other specializations:

- Human osteology, the study of skeletal material. Experts in osteology are able to apply their skills and knowledge to other areas:
  - Paleopathology, which studies the traces of disease and injury in human skeletons
  - Forensic anthropology, the analysis and identification of human remains in the service of coroners or medical examiners. This research often provides law enforcement with important evidence.

Some prominent Physical Anthropologists include the following:

- Davidson Black (1884-1934)
- C. Loring Brace (1930-)
- Robert Broom (1866-1951)
- Carleton S. Coon (1904-1981)
- Raymond Dart (1893-1988)
- Eugene Dubois (1858-1940)
- William Curtis Farabee (1865-1925)
- Sir George Duncan Gibb (1821-1876)
- Ralph L. Holloway (1935-)
- Earnest Hooton (1887-1954)
- F. Clark Howell (1925-)
- Donald C. Johanson (1943-)
- Louis Leakey (1903-1972)
- Mary Leakey (1913-1996)
- Richard Leakey (1944-)
- Pierre Teilhard de Chardin (1881-1955)
- Phillip V. Tobias (1925-)
- Alan C. Walker (1938-)

- Sherwood Washburn (1911-2000)
- Milford H. Wolpoff (1942-)

Paleopathology

Paleopathology is the study of ancient diseases. It is useful in understanding the past history of diseases, and uses this understanding to predict its course in the future.

As such, *paleopathologist* is one who studies old and diseased things, specifically, diseases of human and animal as inferred from recent or fossilized skeletal remains.

First, it is pertinent to note that from the Renaissance to the mid nineteenth century, there was increasing reference to ancient disease, initially within prehistoric animals although later the importance of studying the antiquity of human disease began to be emphasised. The true genesis of the field of human palaeopathology is generally considered to occur between the mid nineteenth century and World War I when a number of pioneering physicians and anthropologists clarified the medical nature of ancient skeletal pathologies. This work was consolidated between the world wars with methods such as radiology, histology and serology being applied more frequently, improving diagnosis and accuracy with the introduction of statistical analysis. It was at this point that palaeopathology can truly be considered to have become a scientific discipline.

Remarkably, after World War II palaeopathology began to be viewed in a different way: as an important tool for the understanding of past populations, and it was at this stage that the discipline began to be related to epidemiology and demography. The study of DNA also began to add new information to what was already known about ancient disease.

Human Paleopathology

Human Osteopathology is classified into several general groups:

(a) Arthropathy

(b) Infection

(c) Oral pathology

(d) Trauma

(e) Tumor

Whilst traumatic injuries such as broken and malformed bones can be easy to spot, evidence of other conditions, for example infectious diseases such as tuberculosis and syphilis, can also be found in bones. Arthropathies, that is joint diseases such as osteoarthritis and gout, are also not uncommon.

Significantly, archaeologists use paleopathology as one of their main tools for understanding the lives of ancient peoples. For example, cranial deformation is evident in the skulls of the Maya, showing that they considered a person beautiful if they had a straight line connecting their nose with their forehead. Another pathology common to Mesoamerica is seen in women. Bone spurs and other deformities in the knees, toes, and backs of women show that their days spent grinding maize to make flour takes its toll on their bodies. Also, evidence for trepanation, or drilling holes in the skull to relieve excess pressure, is also common. Skulls with multiple holes show that some patients survived this procedure many times, because the bone has begun to knit back together.

In archaeology, the study of the diseases of animals has not been as wide and extensive as those of humans. Baker and Brothwell's seminal work was published in 1980 and is still considered a classic text, being frequently referred to within the discipline. However, it should be noted that this position of importance has largely come about, not because of its comprehensive coverage, but because there has been no real alternative. Most palaeopathological literature is to be found in periodicals or compiled publications of conference papers. No synthesis of the research in the field as a whole has been attempted for the last twenty-five years. The study of dinosaur paleopathology has undergone a resurgence in the past two decades.

Current Theories

It is worth while to note that one paper, "The Worst Mistake in the History of the Human Race" and one book, "Paleopathology at the Origins of Agriculture", have been instrumental in bringing about a change in the way prehistoric human history is understood, away from uninformed modernist perceptions skewed by human urban populations' rough times in the dark ages, and more towards an informed and enlightened comprehension of the relative luxury, abundance, and ease of life in pre-agricultural times. One strong proponent of the new conclusions becoming more widely taught and accepted has been John Zerzan, considered by many to be only degrees from an "ecoterrorist", due to his essays bringing to light widespread misinformation in the mainstream understanding of prehistory, and casting a shadow on the relatively recent human "success" of agriculture, evidently causing many readers of his essays to feel something they've chosen to describe as "terror". A few recent books, such as the more popular "Guns, Germs, and Steel", citing paleopathological data, have elicited similar reactions from people.

II

NEUROANTHROPOLOGY

Neuroanthropology is the study of culture and the brain. In one way or another, neuroanthropologists ground their research and explanations in how the human brain develops, how it is structured and how it functions within the genetic limits of its biology (see Biogenetic Structuralism and related website). Interests include the evolution of the hominid brain, cultural development and the brain, the biochemistry of the brain and alternative states of consciousness, human universals, how culture influences perception, how the brain structures experience, so forth.

III

PRIMATOLOGY

Primatology is the study of primates. It is a diverse discipline and primatologists can be found in departments of biology, anthropology, psychology and many others. Physical anthropology is a branch of primatology, which is the primatology of the genus *Homo*, especially *Homo sapiens*. The fields cross over in the study of the hominids, which include all ape-like ancestors of man and the other great apes (for a list of common ancestors with other living species see The Ancestor's Tale).

Modern primatology is an extremely diverse science. It ranges from anatomical studies of primate ancestors and field studies of primates in their natural habitat, to experiments in animal psychology and ape language It has cast an immense amount of light on basic human behaviors and ancient ancestry of these behaviors.

Primatology as a science has many different disciplines that stem from the differing cultural backgrounds of the founders of the field. Indeed, the study itself seems to change throughout different areas of the world, as different approaches, theories and methods are used in the researching of primates and their relationships and links with humans (which are also primates).

There are two main disciplines within the field of primatology, Western primatology and Japanese primatology. These two divergent disciplines stem from their unique cultural backgrounds and philosophies that went into their founding. Although, fundamentally, both Western and Japanese primatology share many of the same principles, the areas of their focus in primate research and their methods of obtaining data differ widely.

Origin

Western primatology stems primarily from colonial research into primate behaviour, especially by French colonial scientists. Early primate study focused primarily in medical research, but some scientists also conducted "civilizing" experiments on chimpanzees in order to gauge both primate intelligence and the limits of their brainpower.

Theory

The Western study of primatology looks at the more biological and psychological aspects of their subjects. Their focus is on studying the common links between humans and primates, past our shield of 'society' and into the nature we share with our ancestors. We will better understand our primitive selves, by understanding our closest animal relatives. Obviously, there have been some cultural and religious issues with the field of primatology, especially as it pertains to the Theory of Evolution.

The discipline of Western primatology is affected by the Judeo-Christian background of European and American science. As such, researchers tend to have a "steward" mentality towards their subjects, much like that of a park ranger or a guardian. Subjects should be unharmed by study, and protected both from and by the research that is done.

Western primatology is a very hard objective science. The general belief is that human interaction with nature must be either extremely limited, or completely controlled. Either way, the observers must be totally neutral to their subjects. This allows for data to be unbiased and for the subjects to be uninfluenced by human interference. This focus relies on two major areas of study; field study – which is the more limited approach – and laboratory study – the more controlled approach. Field study is done in fully natural environments, in which scientific observers literally watch primates exist in their natural habitat. Laboratory study is done in totally controlled lab settings. In this area of study, scientists are able to perform controlled experimentation on the learning capabilities and behavioural patterns of the animals.

Both types of primate study in the Western methodology are meant to be very neutral. Though there are certain Western primatologists who do more subjective research, the emphasis in this discipline is on the objective.

Western primatology tends to focus on individual researchers and their exploits. Stories of researchers such as Dian Fossey and Jane Goodall are extreme examples of this. Long term sites of research tend to be best associated with their founders, and this leads to some tension between younger primatologists and the veterans in the field.

The following list includes the names of some of the prominent Western primatologists

- Geoffrey Bourne
- C.R. Carpenter
- Frans de Waal
- Dian Fossey
- Birute Galdikas
- Dorothy Cheney
- Robert Seyfarth
- Jeanne Altmann
- Richard Wrangham
- Sandy Harcourt
- Marina Cords
- Sue Boinski
- John Mitani
- David Watts
- Tom Struhsaker
- Linda Fedigan
- Colin Chapman
- Meredith Small
- Jane Goodall
- Craig Stanford
- Robert Sapolsky
- Lynne Isbell
- Francine Neago
- Bill McGrew
- Agustin Fuentes

- Karen Strier
- Robert Sussman

Japanese Primatology

Infact the Japanese primatology discipline was developed out of animal ecology. It is mainly credited to Kinji Imanishi and Junichiro Itani. Imanishi was an animal ecologist who began studying wild horses before focusing more on primate ecology. He helped found the Primate Research Group in 1950. Junichiro was a renowned anthropologist and a professor at Kyoto University. He is a co-founder of the Primate Research Institute and the Centre for African Area Studies.

Remarkably, unlike Western Primatology, the Japanese discipline is a male dominated science.

The Japanese discipline of primatology tends to be more interested in the social aspects of primates. Social evolution and anthropology are of primary interest to them. The Japanese theory believes that studying primates will give us insight into the duality of human nature: individual self vs. social self.

The traditional and cultural aspects of Japanese science lend themselves to an "older sibling" mentality. It is believed that animals should be treated with respect, but also a firm authority. This is not to say that the Japanese study of primatology is cruel – far from it – just that it doesn't feel that their subjects should be given reverential treatment.

The noteed Japanese primatologist, Kawai Masao, introduced the concept of *kyokan*. This was the theory that the only way to attain reliable scientific knowledge was to attain a mutual relation, personal attachment and shared life with the animal subjects. Though Kawai is the only Japanese primatologist associated with the use of this term, the underlying principle is part of the foundation of Japanese primate research.

Japanese primatology is a carefully disciplined subjective science. It is believed that the best data comes through identification with your subject. Neutrality is eschewed in favour of a more casual atmosphere, where researcher and subject can mingle more freely. Domestication of nature is not only desirable, but necessary for study. Japanese primatologists are renowned for their ability to recognise animals by sight, and indeed most primates in a research group are usually named and numbered. Comprehensive data on every single subject in a group is uniquely Japanese trait of primate research. Each member of the primate community has a part to play, and the Japanese researchers are interested in this complex interaction.

Mostly for Japanese researchers in primatology, the findings of the team are emphasised over the individual. The study of primates is a group effort, and the group will get the credit for it. It is also not unusual to see a team of researches observing the same group of primates for several years in order to get very detailed demographic and social histories.

Imanishi, Kinji, Junichiro, Itani, and Masao, Kawai are among the renowned Japanese primatologists

Primatology in Sociobiology

It is significant to note that while sociobiology attempts to understand the actions of all animal species within the context of advantageous and disadvantageous behaviors, primatology takes an exclusive look at the order Primates, which includes *Homo sapiens*. The interface between primatology and sociobiology examines in detail the evolution of primate behavioral processes, and what studying our closest living primate relatives can tell about our own minds. As the American anthropologist Earnest Albert Hooton used to say: "Primas sum: primatum nil a me alienum puto" ("I am a primate; nothing about primates is outside of my bailiwick"). The meeting point of these two disciplines has become a nexus of discussion on key issues concerning the evolution of sociality, the development and purpose of language and deceit, and the development and propagation of culture. Additionally, this interface is of particular interest to the science watchers in science and technology studies, who examine the social conditions which incite, mould, and eventually react to scientific discoveries and knowledge. The STS approach to primatology and sociobiology stretches beyond studying the apes, into the realm of observing the people studying the apes.

Before molecular biology, the father of modern taxonomy, Carolus Linnaeus, organized natural objects into kinds. He sorted these kinds by morphology, the shape of the object. As it happens, animals such as chimpanzees and orangutans resemble humans very closely, so Linnaeus placed *Homo sapiens* together with all the other similar-looking organisms into the taxonomic order *Primates*. Modern techniques in molecular biology have reinforced humanity's place within the Primate order. Humans and simians share the vast majority of their DNA, with chimpanzees sharing between 97-99% genetic identity with humans.

Although social grooming is observed in many animal species, the grooming activities undertaken by primates are not strictly for the elimination of parasites. In primates, grooming is a social activity that strengthens relationships.

The amount of grooming taking place between members of a troop is a potent indicator of alliance formation or troop solidarity. Robin Dunbar suggests a link between primate grooming and the development of human language. The size of the neocortex in a primate's brain correlates directly to the number of individuals it can keep track of socially, be it a troop of chimps or a tribe of humans. This number is referred to as the monkeysphere. If a population exceeds the size outlined by its cognitive limitations, the group undergoes a schism. Set into an evolutionary context, the Dunbar number shows a drive for the development of a method of bonding that is less labor intensive than grooming: language. As the monkeysphere grows, the amount of time that would need to be spent grooming troopmates soon becomes unmanageable. Furthermore, it is only possible to bond with one troopmate at a time while grooming. The evolution of vocal communication solves both the time constraint and the one-on-one problem, but at a price. Language allows for bonding with multiple people at the same time at a distance, but the bonding produced by language is less intense. This view of language evolution covers the general biological trends needed for language development, but it takes another hypothesis to uncover the evolution of the cognitive processes necessary for language.

Noam Chomsky's concept of innate language addresses the existence of universal grammar, which suggests a special kind of "device" all humans are born with whose sole purpose is language. Fodor's modular mind hypothesis expands on this concept, suggesting the existence of preprogrammed modules for dealing with many, or all aspects of cognition. Although these modules do not need to be physically distinct, they must be functionally distinct. Orangutans are currently being taught language at the

Smithsonian National Zoo using a computer system developed by primatologist Dr. Francine Neago in conjunction with IBM.

The massive modularity theory thesis posits that there are a huge number of tremendously interlinked but specialized modules running programs called Darwinian algorithms, or DA. DA can be selected for just as a gene can, eventually improving cognition. The contrary theory, of generalist mind, suggests that the brain is just a big computer that runs one program, the mind. If the mind is a general computer, for instance, the ability to use reasoning should be identical regardless of the context. This is not what is observed. When faced with abstract numbers and letters with no "real world" significance, respondents of the Wason card test generally do very poorly. However, when exposed to a test with an identical rule set but socially relevant content, respondents score markedly higher. The difference is especially pronounced when the content is about reward and payment. This test strongly suggests that human logic is based on a module originally developed in a social environment to root out cheaters, and that either the module is at a huge disadvantage where abstract thinking is involved, or that other less effective modules are used when faced with abstract logic.

Further evidence supporting the modular mind has steadily emerged with some startling revelations concerning primates. A very recent study indicated that human babies and grown monkeys approach and process numbers in a similar fashion, suggesting an evolved set of DA for mathematics (Jordan). The conceptualization of both human infants and primate adults is cross-sensory, meaning that they can add 15 red dots to 20 beeps and approximate the answer to be 35 grey squares. As more evidence of basic cognitive modules are uncovered, they will undoubtedly form a more solid foundation upon which the more complex behaviors can be understood.

Primate behavior, like human behavior, is highly social and ripe with the intrigue of kingmaking, powerplays, deception, cuckoldry, and apology. In order to understand the staggeringly complex nature of primate interactions, we look to theory of mind. Theory of mind asks whether or not an individual recognizes and can keep track of information asymmetry amongst individuals in the group, and whether or not they can attribute folk psychological states to their peers. If some primates can tell what others know and want and act accordingly, they can gain advantage and status.

As a recent development, chimpanzee theory of mind has been advanced by Felix Warneken of the Max Planck Institute. His studies have shown that chimpanzees can recognize whether a researcher desires a dropped object, and act accordingly by picking it up. Even more compelling is the observation that chimps will only act if the object is dropped in an accidental-looking manner: if the researcher drops the object in a way that appears intentional, the chimp will ignore the object. In a related experiment, groups of chimps were given rope-pulling problems they could not solve individually.

Warneken's subjects rapidly figured out which individual in the group was the best rope puller and assigned it the bulk of the task. This research is highly indicative of the ability of chimps to detect the folk psychological state of "desire", as well as the ability to recognize that other individuals are better at certain tasks than they are.

As is widely debated scientific studies concerning primate and human behavior have been subject to the same set of political and social complications, or biases, as every other scientific discipline. The borderline and multidisciplinary nature of primatology and sociobiology make them ripe fields of study because they are amalgams of objective and subjective sciences. Current scientific practice, especially in the hard sciences, requires a total dissociation of personal experience from the finished scientific product. This is a strategy that is incompatible with observational field studies, and weakens them in the eyes of hard science.

As mentioned above, the Western school of primatology tries to minimize or control subjectivity to the greatest degree possible, while the Japanese school of primatology tends to embrace the closeness inherent in studying nature. Social critics of science, some operating from within the field, cry foul when reviewing the young disciplines of primatology and sociobiology. Claims are made that researchers form opinions on issues concerning human sociality prior to doing their studies, and then seek evidence that agrees with their worldview or otherwise furthers a sociopolitical agenda. In particular, the use of primatological studies to assert gender roles, and promote or subvert feminism has been a serious point of contention. An example of this is Zuckerman's 1932 study of captive hamadryas baboons, as critiqued in Sturm and Fedigan's Changing Views on Primate Societies. Zuckerman observed male baboons kill each other off in great number in their captive environment. Whether intended or not, the study served to reinforce images of the male as the sole competitor in an often violent race to secure dominance and access to a harem of females. Despite wildly unrealistic overcrowding and completely incorrect male to female ratio, Zuckerman's paper was viewed as good science at the time. These ideas justified the status quo of human male dominance, and consequently, the studies were widely supported and assumed to be the basis of a primate-wide template for behavior, including that of humans.

IV

FORENSIC ANTHROPOLOGY

Basically, forensic anthropology is the application of the science of physical anthropology and human osteology (the study of the human skeleton) in a legal setting, most often in criminal cases where the victim's remains are more or less skeletonized. A forensic anthropologist can also assist in the identification of deceased individuals whose remains are decomposed, burned, mutilated or otherwise unrecognizable. Ethynologically, the adjective "forensic" refers to the application of this subfield of science to a court of law.

There are few people who identify themselves as forensic anthropologists, and in the United States and Canada, there are less than 100 Anthropologists certified as Diplomates of the American Board of Forensic Anthropology. Furthermore, there are only about 50 who are currently active in the field. Most diplomates work in the academic field and consult on casework as it arises.

Infact forensic anthropology borrows methods developed from the academic discipline of physical anthropology and applies them to cases of forensic importance. These techniques can be used to assess age, sex, stature, ancestry, and analyze trauma and disease. Forensic anthropologists frequently work in conjunction with forensic pathologists, odontologists, and homicide investigators to identify a decedent, discover evidence of trauma, and determine the postmortem interval. Though they typically lack the legal authority to declare the official cause of death, their opinions may be taken into consideration by the medical examiner. They may also testify in court as expert witness, though data from some of the techniques commonly used in the field—such as forensic facial reconstruction—are inadmissible as forensic evidence.

A forensic anthropologist may be called in when human remains are found during archaeological excavation, or when badly decomposed, burned, or skeletonized remains are found by law enforcement or members of the public. The identification of skeletal, badly decomposed, or otherwise unidentified human remains is important for both legal and humanitarian reasons. The anthropologist can assess metric and nonmetric characteristics of the bones to determine the minimum number of individuals, sex, stature, age at death, time since death, ancestry and race, health, and unique identifying characteristics such as healed breaks or surgical scars. Sometimes the forensic anthropologist must determine whether the remains found are actually human. Occasionally, positive identification can be established from such remains, but often only an exclusionary identity can be drawn. However, the primary responsibility of a forensic anthropologist is to provide law enforcement with a biological profile of the deceased (age, sex, ancestry, stature, and individualizing characteristics) to help narrow down the possible identity of the decedent.

One vital tool in the assessment of metric skeletal characteristics is the Fordisc program. In skeletal trauma analysis, some forensic anthropologists can accurately determine whether sharp force, blunt force, or ballistic injury occurred before death (antemortem), near the time of death (perimortem), or after death (postmortem). By examining the marks left on bone, particularly skilled forensic anthropologists may be able to determine general class characteristics of the weapon used. Even cremated remains can provide a surprising amount of information about the deceased individual.

Notably Physical anthropology is one of the divisions of the American Academy of Forensic Sciences.

Two of the most important research collections of human skeletal remains in the U.S. are the Hamann-Todd Collection, now housed in the Cleveland Museum of Natural History and the Terry Collection, now housed in the Smithsonian Institution. These collections are an important historic basis for the statistical analysis necessary to make estimates and predictions from found remains. More modern collections include the William M. Bass Donated Skeletal Collection at the University of Tennessee at Knoxville.

The name of some of the renowned anthropologists are furneshed below:

- Thomas Dwight (1843 - 1919)
- Ales Hrdlicka (1869 - 1943)
- Earnest Hooton (1887 - 1954)
- Mildred Trotter (1899 - 1991)
- T. Dale Stewart (1901 - 1997)
- Wilton M. Krogman (1903 - 1987)
- Ellis R. Kerley (1924 - 1998)
- J. Lawrence Angel (1932 - 1988)
- William R. Maples (1937 - 1997)
- Jerome B Bailen (University of the Philippines)

- William M. Bass (University of Tennessee, Emeritus) DABFA
- Sue Black (University of Dundee, UK)
- Sheilagh T. Brooks (University of Las Vegas, Emeritus) DABFA
- Jane E. Buikstra (Arizona State University) DABFA
- Karen Ramey Burns (University of Georgia)
- Emily Craig (author, State Forensic Anthropologist for Kentucky) DABFA
- Dennis C. Dirkmaat (Mercyhurst College) DABFA
- Scott Fairgrieve (Laurentian University, Canada)
- Michael Finnegan (Kansas State University) DABFA
- William Haglund (Physicians for Human Rights)
- Lee Meadows Jantz (University of Tennessee)
- Richard L. Jantz (University of Tennessee, Fordisc)
- Clea Koff (author)
- Kewal Krishan (University of Punjab, India)
- Jerry Melbye (Texas State University, San Marcos) DABFA
- Turhon A. Murad (California State University, Chico) DABFA
- Stephen Ousley (Mercyhurst College, Fordisc)
- Kathy Reichs (author, University of North Carolina) DABFA
- William C. Rodriguez (Armed Forces Institute of Pathology) DABFA

- Clyde Snow (Argentine Forensic Anthropology Team) DABFA
- Marcella Sorg (University of Maine) DABFA
- Judy M. Suchey (Los Angeles Coroner's Office) DABFA
- Steven Symes (Mercyhurst College) DABFA
- Douglas H. Ubelaker (Smithsonian Institution, George Washington University) DABFA
- Jean-Noel Vignal (Centre Technique de la Gendarmerie Nationale)
- Surinder Nath (University of Delhi, India)

V

FORENSIC PATHOLOGY

Forensic pathology is a branch of medicine concerned with determining cause of death, usually for criminal law cases and civil law cases in some jurisdictions. The word forensics is derived from the Latin *forçnsis* meaning *public* or *forum*. The word *pathology* literally means *study of disease*.

Scope

It is significant to note here that the Forensic pathologist:

(a) Is a qualified medical doctor who has completed training in anatomical pathology and who has subsequently sub-specialized in forensic pathology. 'Fully qualified' forensic pathologists are individuals who, for example, are certified by the American Board of Pathology ("board-certified") (United States) or who are eligible for inclusion on the specialist register of the General Medical Council (GMC) having obtained Membership of the Royal College of Pathologists (United Kingdom).

(b) Performs autopsies/ post mortem examinations to determine the cause of death (such as a bullet wound to the head, exsanguination, strangulation, etc.) and (in the USA) the 'manner of death' (for example homicide, accident, natural, suicide or undetermined). The autopsy also provides an opportunity for other issues raised by the death to be addressed, such as the identity of the deceased etc.

(c) Examines wounds and injuries.

(d) Examines tissue specimens under the microscope histology in order to identify the presence or absence of natural disease, as well as to determine the 'age' of wounds and injuries etc.

(e) Interprets toxicological analyses on bodily tissues and fluids to determine e.g. overdoses or deliberate poisonings.

(f) Forensic pathologists also work closely with the medico-legal authority for the area concerned with the investigation of sudden and unexpected deaths i.e. the coroner (England and Wales), Procurator Fiscal (Scotland) or Coroner or medical examiner (United States).

(g) Serves as an expert witness in courts of law testifying in civil or criminal law cases.

In an Autopsy, he /she is often assisted by an autopsy/ mortuary technician (sometimes called a Diener in the USA).

Forensic physicans (sometimes referred to as 'Forensic Medical Examiners' or 'Police Surgeons' (in the UK until recently)) are medical doctors trained in the examination of, and provision of medical treatment to, living victims of assault (including sexual assault) and those individuals who find themselves in police custody. Many forensic physicians in the UK practice clinical forensic medicine on a part-time basis, whilst they also practice family medicine, or another medical specialty.

Investigation of Death

Deaths that are not considered natural are investigated. In some jurisdictions this is done by a *coroner* and in others by a *medical examiner*. In some jurisdictions, the title of "Medical Examiner" is used by non-physician, elected officials involved in medicolegal death investigation. In others, the title is reserved exclusively for physicians that are appointed.

In similar vein, the title "Coroner" is applied to both physicians and non-physicians. Historically, coroners were not all physicians. However, in some jurisdictions the title of "Coroner" is exclusively used by physicians. In Canada, coroners are licensed physicians, usually family physicians.

Infact in, the United States, a coroner, typically, is an elected public official, in a particular geographic jurisdiction, who investigates and certifies deaths. The vast majority of coroners lack a Doctor of Medicine degree and the amount of medical training that they have received is highly variable, depending on their profession (e.g. law enforcement, judges, funeral directors, firefighters, nurses).

In contrast, a medical examiner, typically, is a physician who holds the degree of Doctor of Medicine. Ideally, a medical examiner has completed both a pathology residency (medicine) and a fellowship in forensic pathology.

He or she may also be board certified by the American Board of Pathology in Anatomic and Forensic Pathology.

This entails passing separate examinations in anatomic pathology and forensic pathology. To be eligible for the American Board of Pathology's board examinations, a candidate must demonstrate that he or she has completed training in anatomic pathology and forensic pathology at programs accredited by the Accreditation Council for Graduate Medical Education.

Forensic pathology is a subspecialty of anatomical pathology and typically one year of additional training (a fellowship), that is completed after becoming a licensed anatomical pathologist. Becoming an anatomical pathologist requires completing a four or five year residency in anatomical pathology, which is something one does on completing medical school. In Canada and UK, anatomical pathology is a five year residency. In the US, *anatomic pathology* (as it is called), is a four year residency. In the United States, all told, the education after high school is typically 13 years in duration (4 years undergraduate training + 4 years medical school + 4 years residency (in anatomical pathology) + 1 year forensic pathology fellowship). Generally, the biggest hurdle is gaining admission to medical school.

VI

FORENSIC DENTISTRY

Forensic dentistry or forensic odontology is the proper handling, examination and evaluation of dental evidence, which will be then presented in the interest of justice. The evidence that may be derived from teeth, is the age (in children) and identification of the person to whom the teeth belong. This is done using dental records or ante-mortem (prior to death) photographs. The other type of evidence is that of bite marks, left on either the victim (by the attacker), the perpetrator (from the victim of an attack), or on an object found at the crime scene. Bite marks are often found on children who are abused.

Forensic dentists are responsible for six main areas of practice:

(i) Identification of found human remains

(ii) Identification in mass fatalities

(iii) Assessment of bite mark injuries

(iv) Assessment of cases of abuse (child, spousal, elder)

(v) Civil cases involving malpractice

(vi) Age estimation

Recently, the scientific foundation of forensic odontology, and especially bite mark comparison, has been called into question. An investigative series by the *Chicago Tribune* entitled "Forensics under the Microscope" examined many forensic science disciplines to see if they truly deserve the air of infallibility that has come to surround them. The investigators concluded that bite mark comparison is always subjective and no standards for comparison have been accepted across the field. The journalists discovered that no rigorous experimentation has been conducted to determine error rates for bite mark comparison, a key part of the scientific method. Critics of bite mark comparison cite the case of Ray Krone, an Arizona man convicted of murder on bite mark evidence left on a woman's breast. DNA evidence later implicated another man and Krone was released from prison.

VII

ECOLOGICAL GENETICS

Basically,"Ecological genetics" is the study of genetics on an ecological scale. Whereas molecular genetics studies the structure and function of genes at a molecular level, ecological genetics (and the related field of population genetics) studies phenotypic evolution in natural populations of organisms. Research in this field is of traits of ecological significance — that is, traits related to fitness, which affect an organism's survival and reproduction.

It is worthwhile to note that though work on natural populations had been done previously, it is acknowledged that the field was founded by the Briton E.B. Ford in the early 20th century. *Ecological Genetics* is the title of his 1964 'magnum opus' on the subject. Other notable ecological geneticists would include Theodosius Dobzhansky's work on fruit flies. Ford's genetics school at Oxford in the 1960s is famous for studies, including Bernard Kettlewell's work on the peppered moth. However, obtaining enough data on natural populations was difficult, as was obtaining research grants for long-term projects. As a result, funding was diverted towards molecular genetics. Improved understanding of molecular genetics however, allowed the development of improved biochemical techniques during the 1980s and 1990s which in turn allowed data on natural populations to be derived.

VIII

GENETIC DIVERSITY

Genetic diversity is a characteristic of ecosystems and gene pools that describes an attribute which is commonly held to be advantageous for survival — that there are many different versions of otherwise similar organisms. For example, the Great Irish Famine (1845-1849) can be attributed in part to the fact that the genetic distance of all potatoes in the country was very low, making it easier for one virus to infect and kill much of the crop.

The academic field of population genetics includes several hypotheses regarding genetic diversity. The neutral theory of evolution proposes that diversity is the result of the accumulation of neutral substitutions. Diversifying selection is the hypothesis that two subpopulations of a species live in different environments that select for different alleles at a particular locus. This may occur, for instance, if a species has a large range relative to the mobility of individuals within it. Frequency-dependent selection is the hypothesis that as alleles become more common, they become less fit. This is often invoked in host-pathogen interactions, where a high frequency of a defensive allele among the host means that it is more likely that a pathogen will spread if it is able to overcome that allele.

There are many different ways to measure genetic diversity. The modern causes for the loss of animal genetic diversity have also been studied and identified.

IX

DUAL INHERITANCE THEORY

Dual inheritance theory (DIT), sometimes also known as called gene/culture coevolution, posits that humans are products of the *interaction* between genetic evolution *and* cultural evolution. DIT assumes that culture, (including cultural transmission and cultural evolution), is both influenced by and constrained by genes via psychological adaptations and that culture, in turn, contributes to selection pressures on genes. The results of these interactions can be a mix of both adaptive and maladaptive traits within a population. Another way of conceiving DIT is as an approach that integrates evolutionary theory, cultural theory, and learning theory.

Primarily organic evolutionists began to use mathematical models to investigate the properties of evolution in the first quarter of the 20th Century. The aim of the effort was to take the micro-scale properties of individuals and genes, scale them up to a population of individuals and deduce the long run evolutionary consequences of the assumed micro level processes. Empiricists have a handle on both the micro scale processes and the long run results, but not on what happens over many generations in between. Moreover, human intuition is not so good at envisioning the behavior of populations over long spans of time. As such mathematics proved an invaluable aid.

Evolution and Culture

As a notable development beginning with the pioneering work of Luigi Cavalli-Sforza and Marcus Feldman in the early 1970s, these methods were adapted to study cultural evolution. The problem is considered analogous to that of genetic evolution.

- People acquire information from others by learning and teaching.
- Cultural transmission is imperfect, so the transmission is not always exact.
- People invent new cultural variants, making culture a system for the inheritance of acquired variation.

- People also pick and choose the cultural variants they adopt and use, processes that are not possible in the genetic system (although in the case of sexual selection individuals may choose mates with the objective of getting good genes for their offspring).

Social scientists know a fair amount about such things, enough to build reasonable mathematical representations of the micro-level processes of cultural evolution. The theory is of the form

$$p_{t+1} = p_t + \textit{effects of forces}$$

where p measures something interesting about the culture of a population, for example the fraction of employees who are earnest workers. Teaching and imitation, all else equal, tend to replicate culture. The fraction of workers in a culture who are earnest tends to remain similar from generation to generation. Earnest workers model earnest behavior for others to imitate and try to teach earnestness to new employees. The same can be said for slackers.

Typically, several processes we call forces will act simultaneously to change culture over time. For example, management may find it difficult to discover and punish slacking. Earnest workers may experiment with slacking and find that there are seldom any adverse consequences. Hence, some earnest employees may become slackers. New employees may observe that some people slack and some work hard. They may tend to prefer the easier path.

In the same vein, firms with a high frequency of slackers will tend to fail while those with many earnest workers may prosper. Prosperous firms will have the opportunity to socialize many more new workers than those that fail prematurely. The overall quality of the economy's work force in the long run will be determined by the balance of forces favoring slacking versus those favoring earnestness.

Theorists are interested in the abstract properties of such evolutionary models. Empiricists are interested in finding the models that best describe actual evolving systems. Real world practitioners are interested in predicting the outcomes of policies that might improve or harm the quality of a firm's or an economy's work force.

Substantive questions that have interested dual inheritance theorists include.

(a) the adaptive costs and benefits of culture;
(b) the apparent rarity of cultural learning mechanisms in nature;
(c) the cognitive processes underlying cultural learning and transmission, (i.e. social learning)
(d) the influence of gene-culture coevolution on human psychology and the histories of human societies;
(e) rates of different kinds of cultural evolution;
(f) the evolution of symbolic systems; and
(g) the role of culture in the evolution of cooperation.

Many of the analyses involve the coevolution of genes and culture (hence the term dual inheritance or gene-culture coevolution theory). Genes have an impact on cultural evolution via psychological predispositions that bias what people imitate, teach, or learn for themselves. Hence, a physically awkward type of tool is liable to be modified or abandoned in favor of one that better suits the human hand and arm. The facts that sex is pleasurable, that sweet things taste good, and that being cold and wet is miserable suggest how the structure of our nervous system will have an impact on such things as marriage customs, cuisine, and the construction of shelters.

Cultural influences

However, the opposite is also true. Cultures create environments that in turn may select for genes that succeed in the cultural environment. One of the best worked out cases is adult lactose absorption. In populations with a long history of dairying, such as Northern Europeans and African cattle-keeping societies, most adults retain the ability to break down and hence digest the milk sugar lactose. Societies with no history of dairying, such as East Asians and Amerindians, retain the typical mammalian genotype in which the body shuts down lactase production shortly after the normal age of weaning.

According to some cultural evolutionists our social psychology was extensively remodeled by a long period of life in tribal scale social systems whose culturally transmitted rules encouraged much cooperation with non-relatives due to group selection on cultural variation. Darwin first proposed hypothesis much like this in *The Descent of Man*.

X

POPULATION GENETICS

Basically population genetics is the study of the allele frequency distribution and change under the influence of the four evolutionary forces: natural selection, genetic drift, mutation, gene flow and selective mating. It also takes account of population subdivision and population structure in space. As such, it attempts to explain such phenomena as adaptation and speciation. Population genetics was a vital ingredient in the modern evolutionary synthesis. Sewall Wright, J. B. S. Haldane and R. A. Fisher, were the pioneers in this field who also laid the foundations for the related discipline of quantitative genetics.

Perhaps the most significant "formal" achievement of the modern evolutionary synthesis has been the framework of mathematical population genetics. Indeed some authors (Beatty 1986) would argue that it does *define* the core of the modern synthesis.

Lewontin (1974) outlined the theoretical task for population genetics. He imagined two spaces: a "genotypic space" and a "phenotypic space". The challenge of a *complete* theory of population genetics is to provide a set of laws that predictably map a population of genotypes (G_1) to a phenotype space (P_1), where selection takes place, and another set of laws that map the resulting population (P_2) back to genotype space (G_2) where Mendelian genetics can predict the next generation of genotypes, thus completing the cycle. Even leaving aside for the moment the non-Mendelian aspects revealed by molecular genetics, this is clearly a gargantuan task.

We will refer to this as the "genotype-phenotype map". T^2 is the transformation due to natural selection, T^3 are epigenetic relations that predict genotypes based on the selected phenotypes and finally T^4 the rules of Mendelian genetics.

Practically there are two bodies of evolutionary theory that exist in parallel, traditional population genetics operating in the genotype space and the biometric theory used in plant and animal breeding, operating in phenotype space. The missing part is the mapping between the genotype and phenotype space. This leads to a "sleight of hand" (as Lewontin terms it) whereby variables in the equations of one domain, are considered parameters or *constants*, where, in a full-treatment they would be transformed themselves by the evolutionary process and are in reality *functions* of the state variables in the other domain. The "sleight of hand" is assuming that we know this mapping. Proceeding as if we do understand it is enough to analyze many cases of interest. For example, if the phenotype is almost one-to-one with genotype (sickle-cell disease) or the time-scale is sufficiently short, the "constants" can be treated as such; however, there are many situations where it is inaccurate.

As is said above also, three founders of population genetics were the Britons RA. Fisher and J.B.S. Haldane and the American Sewall Wright. Fisher and Wright had some fundamental disagreements and a controversy about the relative roles of selection and drift continued for much of the century between the Americans and the British. The Frenchman Gustave Malécot was also important early in the development of the discipline. John Maynard Smith was Haldane's pupil, whilst W.D. Hamilton was heavily influenced by the writings of Fisher. The American George R. Price worked with both Hamilton and Maynard Smith. On the American side, Richard Lewontin and the Japanese Motoo Kimura were heavily influenced by Wright. Luigi Luca Cavalli-Sforza is a Stanford-based population geneticist particularly interested in human population genetics.

XI

MICROEVOLUTION

Microevolution is the occurrence of small-scale changes in allele frequencies in a population, over a few generations, also known as change at or below the species level. These changes may be due to several processes: mutation, natural selection, gene flow, genetic drift and nonrandom mating.

Population genetics is the branch of biology that provides the mathematical structure for the study of the process of microevolution. Ecological genetics concerns itself with observing microevolution in the wild. Typically, observable instances of evolution are examples of microevolution; for example, bacterial strains that have antibiotic resistance.

Remarkably, Microevolution can be contrasted with macroevolution; which is the occurrence of large-scale changes in gene frequencies, in a population, over a geological time period (i.e. consisting of extended microevolution). The difference is largely one of approach. Microevolution is reductionist, but macroevolution is holistic. Each approach offers different insights into the evolution process.

Russian Entomologist Yuri Filipchenko (or Philipchenko, depending on the transliteration) first coined the terms "macroevolution" and "microevolution" in 1927 in his German language work, "Variabilität und Variation". The term was brought into English-speaking by Theodosius Dobzhansky in his book Genetics and the Origin of Species (1937). Since the inception of the two two terms, their meanings have been revised several times and even fallen into disfavor amongst scientists who prefer to speak of biological evolution as one process.

XII

QUANTITATIVE GENETICS

First it is pertinent to describe that 'Quantitative genetics' is the study of continuous traits (such as height or weight) and its underlying mechanisms. It is effectively an extension of simple Mendelian inheritance in that the combined effect of the many underlying genes results in a continuous distribution of phenotypic values.

Remarkably, the field quantitative genetics was founded, in evolutionary terms, by the originators of the modern synthesis, R.A. Fisher, Sewall Wright and J.B.S. Haldane, and aimed to predict the response to selection given data on the phenotype and relationships of individuals. Analysis of Quantitative trait loci, or QTL, is a more recent addition to the study of quantitative genetics. A QTL is a region in the genome that affects the trait or traits of interest. Quantitative trait loci approaches require accurate phenotypic, pedigree and genotypic data from a large number of individuals.

It must be remembered that quantitative genetics is not limited to continuous traits, but to all traits that are determined by many genes. This includes:

(a) Continuous traits are quantitative traits with a continuous phenotypic range. They are usually polygenic, and may also have a significant environmental influence.

(b) Meristic trait or other ordinal numbers are expressed in whole numbers, such as number of offspring, or number of bristles on a fruit fly. These traits can be either treated as approximately continuous traits or as threshold traits.

(c) Some qualitative traits can be treated as if they have an underlying quantitative basis, expressed as a threshold trait (or multiple thresholds).

Some human diseases (such as, schizophrenia) have been studied in this manner.

Basic Principles

The phenotypic value (P) of an individual is the combined effect of the genotypic value (G) and the environmental deviation (E):

$$P = G + E$$

The genotypic value is the combined effect of all the genetic effects, including nuclear genes, mitochondrial genes and interactions between the genes. It is therefore often subdivided in an additive (A) and a dominance component (D). The additive effect described the cumulative effect of the individual genes, while the dominance effect is the result of interactions between those genes. The environmental deviation can be subdivided in a pure environmental component (E) and an interaction factor (I) describing the interaction between genes and the environment. This can be described as:

$$P = A + D + E + I$$

The contribution of those components cannot be determined in a single individual, but they can be estimated for whole populations by estimating the variances for those components, denoted as:

$$V_P = V_A + V_D + V_E + V_I$$

The heritability of a trait is the proportion of the total (i.e. phenotypic) variation (V_P) that is explained by the genetic variation. This is the total genetic variation (V_G) in broad sense heritabilities (H^2), while only the additive genetic variation (V_A) is used for narrow sense heritabilities

(h^2), often simply called heritability. The latter gives an indication how a trait will respond to natural or artificial selection.

Central in estimating the variances for the various components is the principle of relatedness. A child has a father and a mother. Consequently, the child and father share 50% of their genes, as do the child and the mother. However, the mother and father normally do not share genes as a result of shared ancestors. Similarly, two full siblings share also on average 50% of the genes with each other, while half sibs share only 25% of the genes. This variation in relatedness can be used to estimate which proportion of the total phenotypic variance (V_p) is explained by the above-mentioned components.

Correlated Traits

Although some genes have only an effect on a single trait, many genes have an effect on various traits. Because of this, a change in a single gene will have an effect on all those traits. This is calculated using covariances, and the phenotypic covariance (Cov_P) between two traits can be partitioned in the same way as the variances described above. The genetic correlation is calculated by dividing the covariance between the additive genetic effects of two traits by the square root of the product of the variances for the additive genetic effects of the two traits:

Osteology

A subdiscipline of anthropology (US) archeology (EU), osteology is a detailed study of the structure of bones, skeletal elements, teeth, morphology, function, disease, pathology, the process of ossification (from cartilaginous molds), the resistance and hardness of bones (biophysics), etc. Often used by scientists with identification of human remains with regard to age, death, gender, growth, and development in a biocultural context.

Remarkably in Osteology, A typical analysis will include:

(a) an inventory of the skeletal elements present
(b) a dental inventory
(c) ageing data, based upon epiphyseal fusion, dental eruption and tooth wear
(d) sexing data, based upon bone morphology
(e) stature and other metric data
(f) race
(g) non-metric traits
(h) pathology and/or cultural modifications
(i) taphonomy, including weathering, gnawing, butchery, burning and related processes

Further, Osteological approaches are frequently applied to investigations in disciplines such as forensic science, physical anthropology and archaeology, and has a place in research on topics including:

- health
- demography
- diet
- disease
- activity patterns
- physique
- genetics of early populations
- population migration
- ancient warfare

- social inequality
- identification of unknown remains
- criminal investigations
- war crimes

Medical Anthropology

Medical anthropology is a sub-branch of anthropology that is concerned with the application of anthropological and social science theories and methods to questions about health, illness and healing. Some medical anthropologists are trained primarily in anthropology as their main discipline, while others have studied anthropology after training and working in health or related professions such as medicine, nursing or psychology. Medical anthropologists conduct research in settings as diverse as rural villages and urban hospitals and clinics. They may teach medical anthropology in university anthropology departments, medical and nursing schools and in community-based settings.

The main themes and questions in medical anthropology include:

- Development of systems of medical knowledge and health care
- Patient-practitioner relationships
- Integrating alternative medical systems in culturally diverse environments
- The interactions between biological, environmental and social factors influencing health and illness at both individual and community levels
- The impacts of biomedicine and biomedical technologies in non-Western settings

Paleoethnobotany

Paleoethnobotany, also known as archaeobotany in European (particularly British) academic circles, is the archaeological sub-field that studies plant remains from archaeological sites. The major research themes are recovery and identification of plant remains, the use of wild plants, the origins of agriculture and domestication, and the co-evolution of human-plant interactions.

Paleoethnobotanists use a variety of methods to identify and recover plant remains. One method is to sieve excavated material in a water bath in order to allow the organic material to float to the surface. This method is known as *flotation.* The matrix (the soil from a suspected archaeological feature) is slowly added to agitated water. The soil, sand, and other heavy material, known as *heavy fraction*, will sink to the bottom. The less dense organic material such as charred seeds, wood and bone will tend to float to the surface. The material that floats to the top, called *light fraction*, is gathered with a sieve. The organic light fraction is then available for examination. Samples of the heavy fraction are also gathered for later analysis.

Another method used by paleoethnobotanists is the reconstitution and analysis of human paleofeces (sometimes the term coprolite is used).

A related field is palynology — the study of pollens. This has been used by many scientific disciplines. For paleoethnobotanists, it is a search for clues to early human environments and diet.

Another discipline used by paleoethnobotanists is dendrochronology.

The work done in paleoethnobotany can be divided into

field work, collections management, systematic description of species, and theories into the origins of human and plant interaction. A paleoethnobotanist may find discrete concentrations of burned or dried remnants of seeds in an area of discolored soil (a possible hearth feature). If later analyses indicate that the remnants were of only mature wild seeds of a type of plant that grows locally, it could be inferred that the site was only visited seasonally. Such an inference could be supported by a lack of other features that would suggest that no permanent shelters were built at the site.

Alternatively, a paleoethnobotanist may find that a fire pit feature contains concentrated remnants of a wide variety of edible wild plants that mature throughout the year. An archaeologist may find features at the site that indicate some sort of semi-permanent dwellings (such as post holes and middens). The middens may have concentrations of animal remains, identified by a zooarchaeologist as those of wild game, with a variety of species-specific maturity levels. In that case, a more permanent settlement may be inferred, perhaps to the level of a village. Such an analysis of the archaeological features could suggest a society of hunter-gatherers who inhabited the site on a more-or-less year-round basis. A paleoethnobotanist may also find concentrated remains of plants that typically are only grown through active cultivation (such as corn, beans, and squash). At the same site, an archaeologist might identify features such as stone walls surrounding enclosures arrayed in a pattern, and deep, layered middens with concentrations of domesticated animal remains such as goats or pigs. An analysis of the site, set within the context of the archaeological features and animal and plant remains, would suggest a settled agrarian community.

Paleoanthropology

Basically, as a field of studies Paleoanthropology is the branch of physical anthropology (often called biological anthropology) that focuses on the study of human evolution, tracing the anatomic, behavioral and genetic linkages of pre-humans from millions of years ago up to modern times. Paleoanthropologists study early hominids through fossil remains, traces, or impressions of ancient life; evidence such as preserved bones, tools, or footprints. Typically, a team is composed of scientists, students, and local workers, representing diverse backgrounds and academic fields.

According to Ian Tattersall paleoanthropology is distinguished as the "branch of science [that] keeps its primary data secret," it is perhaps more accurate to observe that primary physical evidence in paleoanthropology is among the most difficult to obtain.

Historical Development

It is worthwhile to mention that the modern field of paleoanthropology began in the 19th century with the discovery of "Neanderthal man" (the eponymous skeleton was found in 1856, but there had been finds elsewhere since 1830), and with evidence of so-called cave men. The idea that humans are similar to certain great apes had been obvious to people for some time, but the idea of the biological evolution of species in general was not legitimized until after Charles Darwin published *On the Origin of Species* in 1859. Though Darwin's first book on evolution did not address the specific question of human evolution— "light will be thrown on the origin of man and his history," was all Darwin wrote on the subject— the implications of evolutionary theory were clear to contemporary readers.

Debates between Thomas Huxley and Richard Owen focused on the idea of human evolution. Huxley convincingly illustrated many of the similarities and differences between humans and apes in his 1863 book *Evidence as to Man's Place in Nature*. By the time Darwin published his own book on the subject, *Descent of Man*, it was already a well-known interpretation of his theory— and the interpretation which made the theory highly controversial. Even many of Darwin's original supporters (such as Alfred Russel Wallace and Charles Lyell) balked at the idea that human beings could have evolved their apparently boundless mental capacities and moral sensibilities through natural selection.

Remarkably, since the time of Carolus Linnaeus, the great apes were considered the closest relatives of human beings, based on morphological similarity. In the 19th century, it was speculated that their closest living relatives were chimpanzees and gorillas, and based on the natural range of these creatures, it was surmised humans share a common ancestor with African apes and that fossils of these ancestors would ultimately be found in Africa.

However, prior to today's general acceptance of Africa as the root of genus *Homo,* 19th century naturalists sought after the origin of man in Asia. The recognition of human antiquity in the Far East was, of course, the fruit of Eugene Dubois' fervent pursuit in Indonesia for the missing link (between ape and man) and the subsequent discovery and naming of *Pithecanthropus erectus* near the Solo River on Java in the 1890s.

For a long time, western scholars were knowledgeable of the so-called "dragon bones" (fossil bones and teeth) from the Chinese apothecary shops. It was not until the early 1900s, however, that German paleontologist, Max

Schlosser, first described a single human tooth from Beijing. Although Schlosser (1903) was very cautious, identifying the tooth only as "?*Anthropoide g. et sp. indet*?," he was hopeful that future work would discover a new anthropoid in China.

Fast-forward 11 years, enter the Swedish geologist Johan Gunnar Andersson. Andersson was sent to China as a mining advisor, but he soon developed a passion for the "dragon bones." It was he who, in 1918, discovered the sites around Zhoukoudian, a village about 50 kilometers southwest of Beijing proper. However, because of the sparse nature of the initial finds, the site was inevitably abandoned. Work did not resume again until 1921, when the Austrian paleontologist, Otto Zdansky, fresh with his doctoral degree from Vienna, came to Beijing to work for Andersson. Zdansky conducted short-term excavations at Locality 1 in 1921 and 1923, and recovered only two teeth of significance (one premolar and one molar) that he subsequently described, cautiously, as "?*Homo sp.*". With that done, Zdansky returned to Austria and suspended all fieldwork.

Curprisingly, the news of the fossil hominin teeth delighted the scientific community in Beijing, and plans soon began to formulate aimed at developing a larger, more systematic project at Zhoukoudian. At the epicenter of excitement was Davidson Black, a Canadian-born anatomist working at the Peking Union Medical College. Black shared Andersson's interest, as well as his view that central Asia was a promising home for early humankind. In late 1926, Black channeled a formal proposal through the Union Medical College to the Rockefeller Foundation concerning financial support for the systematic excavation at Zhoukoudian, and the establishment of an institute for the study of human biology in China.

The Zhoukoudian Project came to existence in the spring of 1927, and two years later, the Cenozoic Research Laboratory of the Geological Survey of China was formally established. Being the first institution of its kind, the Cenozoic Laboratory opened up new avenues for the studies of paleogeology and paleontology in China. Moreover, the Laboratory was the precursor of the Institute of Vertebrate Paleontology and Paleoanthropology (IVPP) of the Chinese Academy of Science, of which took its modern form after 1949. The first of the major project finds should be attributed to the young Swedish paleontologist, Anders Birger Bohlin, then serving as the Field Advisor at Zhoukoudian. He recovered a left, lower molar which Black (1927) identified as unmistakably human (it compared favorably to the previous find made by Zdansky), and subsequently coined it [[*Sinanthropus pekinensis*]], Black and Zdansky 1927. The news was at first met with skepticism, and many scholars had reservations that a single tooth was sufficient to justify the naming of a new type of early hominin. Yet within a little more than two years, in the winter of 1929, Pei Wenzhong, then the Field Director of Zhoukoudian, unearthed the first, complete calvaria of Peking Man. Twenty-seven years after Schlosser's initial description, the antiquity of early humans in East Asia was no longer a speculation, but a reality.

Further excavations continued at the site and remained fruitful until the outbreak of the Sino-Japanese War in 1937. The decade long research yielded a wealth of faunal and lithic materials, as well as hominin fossils. These included 5 more complete calvaria, 9 large cranial fragments, 6 facial fragments, 14 partial mandibles, 147 isolated teeth, and 11 postcranial elements-estimated to represent as least 40 individuals. Evidence of fire, marked by ash lenses and burned bones and stones, were apparently also present (Black, 1931), albeit recent studies have challenged this view (Weiner et al., 1998; Weiner et al., 1999). Franz Weidenreich came to Beijing soon after Black's untimely death in 1934, and took over the academic affairs of studying the hominin specimens.

Unfortunately, following the tragic loss of the Peking Man materials in late 1941, scientific endeavors at Zhoukoudian and elsewhere slowed. For the most part, it was because of the lack of funding. Conversely, frantic search for the missing fossils also figured prominently, and efforts continued well into the 1950s. Nonetheless, after the establishment of the People's Republic of China in 1949, excavations resumed at Zhoukoudian. But as the story goes, with political instability and social unrest brewing in China, beginning in 1966, and major discoveries at Olduvai Gorge and East Turkana (Koobi Fora), the paleoanthropological spotlights inevitably shifted westward to East Africa. While China re-opened its doors to the West in the late 1970s, national policy calling for self-reliance, coupled with a widened language barrier, thwarted all the possibilities of renewed scientific relationships.

Back in South Africa, a notable and rare find came to light in 1924. In a cave site at Taung, Professor Raymond Dart discovered a remarkably well-preserved juvenile specimen (face and brain endocast) and named it *Australopithecus africanus* (*Australopithecus* = Souther Ape). Although the brain was small (410 cm^3), its shape was rounded, unlike that of chimpanzees and gorillas, and more like a modern human brain. In addition, the specimen exhibited short canine teeth, and the foramen magnum was more anteriorly placed, hinting a bipedal mode of locomotion. All of these traits convinced Dart that the

Taung child was a bipedal human ancestor, a transitional form between ape and man. Another 20 years would pass before Dart's claims were taken seriously, following the discovery of additional australopith fossils in Africa that resemble his type specimen. The prevailing view of the time was that a large brain evolved before bipedality. It was thought that intelligence on par with modern humans was a prerequisite to bipedalism.

Currently, the australopiths are considered to be the last common ancestors leading to genus *Homo*, the group to which modern humans belong. Both australopiths and *Homo sapiens* are part of the tribe Hominini, but recent morphological data have brought into doubt the position of *A. africanus* as a direct ancestor of modern humans; it may well have been a dead-end cousin. The australopiths were originally grouped based on size as either gracile or robust. The robust variety of *Australopithecus* has since been renamed as *Paranthropus* (*P. robustus* from South Africa, and *P. boisei* and *P. aethiopicus* from East Africa). In the 1930s, when the robust specimens were first described, the *Paranthropus* genus was used. During the 1960s, the robust variety was moved into *Australopithecus*. The recent consensus has been back to the original classification as a separate genus.

7

TRIBALS (ADIVASIS) OF INDIA

Adivasis, literally autochtones, i.e. "original people of the forest", comprise a substantial indigenous minority of the population of India. Indian tribals are also called Atavika (forest dwellers, in Sanskrit texts), Vanvasis or Girijans (hill people, e.g. by Mahatma Gandhi). Tribal peoples are particularly numerous in the Indian states of Orissa, Madhya Pradesh, Chattisgarh, Rajasthan, Gujarat, Maharashtra, Andhra Pradesh, Bihar, Jharkhand, West Bengal and in extreme northeastern states such as Mizoram. Officially they are recognized by the Indian government as "Scheduled Tribes" in the Fifth Schedule of the Constitution of India. Under the influence and by tiresome efforts of Christian Missionaries from Europe and the USA during the 19th century, substantial numbers converted to Christianity.

Many smaller tribal groups are quite sensitive to ecological degradation caused by modernization. Both commercial forestry and intensive agriculture have proved destructive to the forests that had endured swidden agriculture for many centuries.

There were several Adivasis in the Indian independence

movement including Khajya Naik, Bhima Naik, Jantya Bhil and Rehma Vasave.

It is wothwhile to mention that demographically, tribal peoples constitute 8.3% of the India's total population, over 84 million people according to the 2001 census. Remarkably, the geographical distribution of tribal is great by uneven. One concentration lives in a belt along the Himalayas stretching through Jammu and Kashmir, Himachal Pradesh, and Uttarakhand in the west, to Assam, Meghalaya, Tripura, Arunachal Pradesh, Mizoram, Manipur, and Nagaland in the northeast. Remarkably, in the northeastern states of Arunachal Pradesh, Meghalaya, Mizoram, and Nagaland, a majority of (i.e. over 90% of the population is tribal. However, in the remaining northeast states of Assam, Manipur, Sikkim, and Tripura, tribal peoples form between 20 and 30% of the population.

Another concentration lives in the hilly areas of central India (Chhattisgarh, Madhya Pradesh, Orissa, and, to a lesser extent in, Andhra Pradesh); in this belt, which is bounded by the Narmada River to the north and the Godavari River to the southeast, tribal peoples occupy the slopes of the region's mountains. Other tribals, including the Santals, live in Jharkhand and West Bengal. Central Indian states have the country's largest tribes, and, taken as a whole, roughly 75% of the total tribal population live there, although the tribal population there accounts for only around 10% of the region's total population.

Further there are smaller numbers of tribal people in Karnataka, Tamil Nadu, and Kerala in south India; in western India in Gujarat and Rajasthan, and in the union territories of Lakshadweep and the Andaman Islands and Nicobar Islands. About one percent of the populations of

Kerala and Tamil Nadu are tribal, whereas about six percent tribals are there in Andhra Pradesh and Karnataka.

Who are Tribals?

Actually there is no unanimity about classifying a community as tribe. This problem has complex due to politicians as apart from the use of strictly legal criteria, however, the problem of determining which groups and individuals are tribal is both subtle and complex. Because it concerns economic interests and voting blocs, the question of who are members of Scheduled Tribes rather than Backward Classes or Scheduled Castes is often controversial. This is evident from the unrest perpetrated by Gujjars of Rajasthan recently in May 2007, demanding ST status.

A number of traits have customarily been seen as establishing tribal rather than caste identity. These include language, social organization, religious affiliation, economic patterns, geographic location, and self-identification. Recognized tribes typically live in hilly regions somewhat remote from caste settlements; they generally speak a language recognized as tribal.

Unlike castes, which form part of a complex and interrelated local economic exchange system, tribes tend to form self-sufficient economic units. For most tribal people, land-use rights traditionally derive simply from tribal membership. Tribal society tends to the egalitarian, with its leadership based on ties of kinship and personality rather than on hereditary status. Tribes typically consist of segmentary lineages whose extended families provide the basis for social organization and control. Tribal religion recognizes no authority outside the tribe. Any of these criteria may not apply in specific instances. Language does not always give an accurate indicator of tribal or caste status. Especially in regions of mixed population, many tribal groups have lost their mother tongues and simply speak local or regional languages. In parts of Assam - an area historically divided between warring tribes and villages - increased contact among villagers began during the colonial period, and has accelerated since independence in 1947. A pidgin Assamese developed while educated tribal members learned Hindi and, in the late twentieth century, English.

Self-identification and group loyalty do not provide unfailing markers of tribal identity either. In the case of stratified tribes, the loyalties of clan, kin, and family may well predominate over those of tribe. In addition, tribes cannot always be viewed as people living apart; the degree of isolation of various tribes has varied tremendously. The Gonds, Santals, and Bhils traditionally have dominated the regions in which they have lived. Moreover, tribal society is not always more egalitarian than the rest of the rural populace; some of the larger tribes, such as the Gonds, are highly stratified.

The apparently wide fluctuation in estimates of South Asia's tribal population through the twentieth century gives a sense of how unclear the distinction between tribal and nontribal can be. India's 1931 census enumerated 22 million tribal people, in 1941 only 10 million were counted, but by 1961 some 30 million and in 1991 nearly 68 million tribal members were included. The differences among the figures reflect changing census criteria and the economic incentives individuals have to maintain or reject classification as a tribal member.

These gyrations of census data serve to underline the complex relationship between caste and tribe. Although, in theory, these terms represent different ways of life and ideal types, in reality they stand for a continuum of social groups. In areas of substantial contact between tribes and castes, social and cultural pressures have often tended to move tribes in the direction of becoming castes over a period of years. Tribal peoples with ambitions for social advancement in Indian society at large have tried to gain the classification of caste for their tribes. On occasion, an entire tribe or part of a tribe joined a Hindu sect and thus entered the caste system *en masse*. If a specific tribe engaged in practices that Hindus deemed polluting, the tribe's status when it was assimilated into the caste hierarchy would be affected.

As a recent development, the economic privilages being availed by ST people have lured the caste people to have the tribal status. Since independence, however, the special benefits available to Scheduled Tribes have convinced many groups, even Hindus and Muslims, that they will enjoy greater advantages if so designated. The schedule gives tribal people incentives to maintain their identity. By the same token, the schedule also includes a number of groups whose 'tribal' status, in cultural terms, is dubious at best.

Tribals and Hinduism

Some Hindus believe that Indian tribals are close to the romantic ideal of the ancient silvan culture of the Vedic people. The founder RSS Golwalkar said: "The tribals "can be given yajñopavîta (secred chread of Hindus) They should be given equal rights and footings in the matter of religious rights, in temple worship, in the study of Vedas, and in general, in all our social and religious affairs. This is the only right solution for all the problems of casteism found nowadays in our Hindu society."

At the Lingaraja temple in Bhubaneswar (11th century), there are Brahmin and Badu (tribal) priests. The Badus have the most intimate contact with the deity of the temple, and only they can bathe and adorn it.

There were also tribal reform and rebellion movements during the period of the British Empire, some of which also participated in the Indian freedoom struggle or attacked mission posts.

The Bhil tribe is mentioned in the epic Mahabharata. The Bhil boy Eklavya's teacher was Drona, and he had the honour to be invited to Yudhisthira's Rajasuya Yajna at Indraprastha. Indian tribals were also part of royal armies in the Ramayana and in the Arthasastra. Bhakta Shabari was a Bhil woman that offered Shri Rama and Shri Laxmana 'ber'(a wild gruit) when they were searching for Shri Sita in the forest. Maharishi Matanga, a Bhil became a Brahmana.

Tribal System

Basically, Tribal are not part of caste system. This is an eglitarian society. Christian tribals do not automatically lose their traditional tribal rules. When in 1891 a missionary asked 150 Munda Christians to inter-dine with people of different rank, only 20 Christians did so, and many converts lost their new faith. Father Haghenbeek concluded on this episode that these rules are not "pagan", but a sign of "national sentiment and pride", and wrote: "On the contrary, while proclaiming the equality of all men before God, we now tell them: preserve your race pure, keep your customs, refrain from eating with Lohars (blacksmiths), Turis (bamboo workers) and other people of lower rank. To become good Christians, it (inter-dining) is not required."

Extending the system of primary education into tribal

areas and reserving places for tribal children in middle and high schools and higher education institutions are central to government policy, but efforts to improve a tribe's educational status have had mixed results. Recruitment of qualified teachers and determination of the appropriate language of instruction also remain troublesome. Commission after commission on the "language question" has called for instruction, at least at the primary level, in the students' native tongue. In some regions, tribal children entering school must begin by learning the official regional language, often one completely unrelated to their tribal tongue.

Many tribal schools are plagued by high dropout rates. Children attend for the first three to four years of primary school and gain a smattering of knowledge, only to lapse into illiteracy later. Few who enter continue up to the tenth grade; of those who do, few manage to finish high school. Therefore, very few are eligible to attend institutions of higher education, where the high rate of attrition continues. Members of agrarian tribes like the Gonds often are reluctant to send their children to school, needing them, they say, to work in the fields. On the other hand, in those parts of the northeast where tribes have generally been spared the wholesale onslaught of outsiders, schooling has helped tribal people to secure political and economic benefits. The education system there has provided a corps of highly trained tribal members in the professions and high-ranking administrative posts. Meenas of Rajasthan and Bhotias of Uttarakhand are glaring example of this who have availed the education fruitfully.

Tribal Economy

Geographically, most tribes are concentrated in heavily forested areas that combine inaccessibility with limited political or economic significance. Historically, the economy of most tribes was subsistence agriculture or hunting and gathering. Tribal members traded with outsiders for the few necessities they lacked, such as salt and iron. A few local Hindu craftsmen might provide such items as cooking utensils.

However, the early 20th century, large areas fell into the hands of non-tribals, on account of improved transportation and communications. Around 1900, many regions were opened by the government to settlement through a scheme by which inward migrants received ownership of land free in return for cultivating it. For tribal people, however, land was often viewed as a common resource, free to whoever needed it. By the time tribals accepted the necessity of obtaining formal land titles, they had lost the opportunity to lay claim to lands that might rightfully have been considered theirs. The colonial and post-independence regimes belatedly realized the necessity of protecting tribals from the predations of outsiders and prohibited the sale of tribal lands. Although an important loophole in the form of land leases was left open, tribes made some gains in the mid-twentieth century, and some land was returned to tribal peoples despite obstruction by local police and land officials.

In the 1970s, tribal peoples came again under intense land pressure, especially in central India. Migration into tribal lands increased dramatically, as tribal people lost title to their lands in many ways – lease, forfeiture from debts, or bribery of land registry officials. Other non-tribals simply squatted, or even lobbied governments to classify them as tribal to allow them to compete with the formerly established tribes. In any case, many tribal members became landless labourers in the 1960s and 1970s, and regions that a few years earlier had been the exclusive domain of tribes had an increasingly mixed population of tribals and non-tribals. Government efforts to evict nontribal members from illegal occupation have proceeded slowly; when evictions occur at all, those ejected are usually members of poor, lower castes.

Infact improved communications, roads with motorized traffic, and more frequent government intervention figured in the increased contact that tribal peoples had with outsiders. Commercial highways and cash crops frequently drew non-tribal people into remote areas. By the 1960s and 1970s, the resident nontribal shopkeeper was a permanent feature of many tribal villages. Since shopkeepers often sell goods on credit (demanding high interest), many tribal members have been drawn deeply into debt or mortgaged their land. Merchants also encourage tribals to grow cash crops (such as cotton or castor-oil plants), which increases tribal dependence on the market for basic necessities. Indebtedness is so extensive that although such transactions are illegal, traders sometimes 'sell' their debtors to other merchants, much like indentured peons. The final blow for some tribes has come when nontribals, through political jockeying, have managed to gain legal tribal status, that is, to be listed as a Scheduled Tribe.

It is remarkable have to mention that tribes in the Himalayan foothills have not been as hard-pressed by the intrusions of non-tribals. Historically, their political status was always distinct from the rest of India. Until the British colonial period, there was little effective control by any of the empires centred in peninsular India; the region was populated by autonomous feuding tribes. The British, in efforts to protect the sensitive northeast frontier, followed a policy dubbed the "Inner Line"; nontribal people were allowed into the areas only with special permission. Post Independence governments have continued the policy, protecting the Himalayan tribes as part of the strategy to secure the border with China.

Further government policies on forest reserves have massively affected tribal peoples. Government efforts to reserve forests have precipitated armed (if futile) resistance on the part of the tribal peoples involved. Intensive exploitation of forests has often meant allowing outsiders to cut large areas of trees (while the original tribal inhabitants were restricted from cutting), and ultimately replacing mixed forests capable of sustaining tribal life with single-product plantations. Nontribals have frequently bribed local officials to secure effective use of reserved forest lands which is a common practice in India.

The northern tribes have thus been sheltered from the kind of exploitation that those elsewhere in South Asia have suffered. In Arunachal Pradesh, for example, tribal members control commerce and most lower-level administrative posts. Government construction projects in the region have provided tribes with a significant source of cash. Some tribes have made rapid progress through the education system (the role of early missionaries was significant in this regard). Instruction was begun in Assamese but was eventually changed to Hindi; by the early 1980s, English was taught at most levels. Northeastern tribal people have thus enjoyed a certain measure of social mobility.

Prominent Scheduled Tribes

- Andamanese
- Bhils
- Bhotias/Bhutia

- Buxa
- Dhodia Tribes of Gujarat
- Gonds
- Khasis
- Indigenous people of Lakshadweep
- Jabhnsaris
- Kurichiya
- Kurumbar
- Tripuris
- Mizos
- Mundaris
- Nagas
- Nicobarese
- Oraon
- Santals
- Todas
- Maldharis of Gujarat.
- Cholanaikkan
- Warli
- Kisan Tribe

Towards Development

Consequent upon the contact with the non-tribal world, wide socio-economic differences are observed in the tribal population. Tribal groups around industrial and urban complexes have different problems from their brothers who live in comparative isolation. Religious conversion has added another factor of differentiation into the tribal way of life. Considering these factors of differentiation in their eco-systems, traditional economic pursuits, beliefs and practices, and recent industrial and urban impacts, Vidyarthi (1975) classifies the tribal population of India into six occupational types. These are: (1) hunters and food-gatherers, (2) hill cultivators, (3) plains farmers, (4) simple artisans, (5) cattle-keepers, and (6) industrial urban workers.

In the context of a specific area or tribe this classification can be suitably modified. Since each type is likely to have a life-style of its own, it is suggested that an approach to development should be "type" oriented and not tribe oriented. The latter is likely to oversimplify a very complicated situation and deflect the aims of development from reality. Schemes for development should be conceived and developed within sociocultural norms of the community based on micro-level plan parameters. Plans conceived in terms of the tribe as a whole may not be useful when the tribe has a huge population so that sections thereof live in different States, or even in different countries under widely different environmental conditions.

It is pertinent to note that most tribals, to whatever occupational type they belong, are below the poverty line. They are highly in debt. A major part of their earnings goes to the money-lenders and other exploiters who impose upon the tribal simplicity and ignorance. The poverty of tribal India is glaring. Poverty, however, should not be taken to mean only food, quantitatively and qualitatively, but also ignorance, illiteracy, immobility, unhygienic living conditions, suffering from easily curable diseases, early death and the like.

Micro-level planning shall lead to the discovery of priorities of each community. It may be necessary to give education top priority for one community, whereas, someone else may demand immediate freedom from the clutches of unscrupulous traders and money-lenders; and still another may require health care measures, to start with. The approach inevitably requires a thorough *a priori* survey and assessment of the needs of the community together with an understanding of its cultural base. Non-understanding of the cultural background of the community has, in the past, led to the failure of many well-meaning developmental measures. To this category belongs the scheme of putting up colonies to provide houses with farmland to tribal groups. A typical case may be referred to:

Somewhere in Kurnool district the Government of Andhra Pradesh built a colony with a provision for houses, farmland, etc., to accommodate 100 forest-dwelling, food-gathering Chenchu families. The non-agricultural Chenchu population was never attracted towards this, proposed farming life. As a result "one cannot even recognise the signs of the colony that existed once" (Reddy, 1976). Cases reported from West Bengal are not much different from the Chenchu case (Bhowmick, 1975). The Commissioner for Scheduled Castes and Scheduled Tribes has recorded a number of cases of failure of colonising schemes in his tenth report. The failure is attributed to the divergence of the colony way of life from the cherished cultural values of the communities involved.

Concern for the uplift and development of the tribal population has been shown mainly by social workers and governmental agencies. Though a large number of individuals and organisations in the former category are very active in certain localities of the country, they have not been able either to coordinate their efforts or to measure up to the problem involved. Therefore initiative to development and change has come to be regarded as an urgent and pressing governmental responsibility. It is deliberately pursued and consciously oriented towards quick results to be in tune with the general economic policy of the nation. This, most often, is unfortunately formulated on the basis of inadequate and fragmentary data. The planners make costly mistakes. Consequently, the development policy has led to the creation of impossible expectations and, therefore, inevitable disappointments.

In fact, approach to tribal development suggested by the anthropologists requires clear *a priori* understanding of the social organisation and cultural values through sustained field investigation, collection of adequate and complete data before planning and formulating any policy of development for any group of people. There is no single cause for economic under-development or cultural stagnation. Many forces, economic, social, political, religious, historical and cultural which at certain points of time may be mutually reinforcing and at certain others mutually contradictory, are at work.

Practically, no single social science can provide all the data or conceptual apparatus necessary to identify, analyse and understand the problems of tribes who are at different levels of technological, economic and cultural development. The anthropological approach suggests need to involve specialists from all fields of study relevant for development including social workers and administrators.

Anthropology can provide adequate data to identify cultural forces: That does not seem to be enough to formulate an infallible policy for development. The planner should be provided with the all necessary data regardless of which sector of social reality they come from. The analysts must identify all relevant forces at work so that integrative forces of the culture of the group considered for development can possibly be used as effective tools; headon collision with resistant spots of tribal life can be tactfully avoided and the people can be pursued to associate effectively with the development programmes rather than remaining either as passive and indifferent onlookers or offering active resistance.

Most unfortunately, the anthropologist is the most misunderstood social scientist in the context of tribal policy in India. The genesis of this misunderstanding is traced to the policy suggested for the North-East Frontier region of the country by Elwin (1975). Elwin (1964 45-46), however, refers to a debate in the Legislative Assembly on the Excluded Areas, sometimes in February 1936, where "a number of speakers attacked anthropologists as wishing to keep the primitive people of India 'uncivilised' and 'in a state of barbarism' in order to add 'to their blessed stock of scientific knowledge". He wonders "how this curious idea arose". He had, no doubt, advocated a policy of temporary isolation for certain small tribes when India was under British rule. This was not to keep them as they were "but because at that time the only contacts they had with the outside world were debasing contacts, leading to economic exploitation and cultural destruction. Nothing positive was being done for their welfare. National workers were not admitted to their hills, but merchants, moneylenders, landlords and liquor-venders were working havoc with their economy and the missionaries were destroying their art, their dances, their weaving and their whole culture".

The policy of temporary isolation followed towards the tribal population of Arunachal Pradesh has borne excellent results where tribesmen now are able to interact with the outside world with confidence and ease. No anthropologist has ever suggested a policy of complete isolation for the tribal population and would never dream of suggesting such a policy. The most fundamental position taken by Elwin in his "Philosophy for NEFA" which, by and large, is accepted by the rest in the profession is to "approach the tribesman with the mind of the tribesman"; not to look upon the tribal folk as "specimens", but as people, as human beings "exactly like ourselves in all fundamental ways". No doubt, "they live under special conditions; they have developed along certain special lines; they have their own outlook and ways of doing things. But the ultimate human needs, aspirations, loves and fears are exactly the same as ours" (Elwin, 1964).

Tribals in Transition

The modern faith stems from an axiomatic certainty of immense consequence. The grand certainty is that the continually enhanced human capacity to reshape the material world is an unfailing assurance of human liberation and freedom. Progress is the sovereign quest of modern civilisation as also its cardinal referent for meaning and significance. Hence the perception that tribal cohesions represent the survival of archaic social formations which the ever expanding reach of the modern historical process would in time transform and completely recast.

And true enough, the power to reshape the material world has linked and unified the most distant corners of the earth. But for communities and rhythms of life, towards which words like tribe direct our attention, modern unification has meant a virtual half-life on the very margins of modern life and discourse. Consider in this context the intellectual and cultural lineage of the discipline of Ethnology. Its origin and orientation are unmistakably modern. Its mission is to understand and make sense of social facts and forms of thought that clearly do not belong to the modern universe. Levi-Strauss sensed in ethnology a belated sence of remorse. As an intellectual artifact it is inherently ambiguous. It seeks remembrance for facts and forms, which it knows, are marked out for extinction by the very mode of doing and thinking from which ethnology arises. Recognition of definitive difference constitutes as it were its formative substance. And all the while, it knows, that this difference has at best a bleak future in the modern world. In its rare moments of repose modern thought invests rhythms of living forsaken by history, in the words of Levi-Strauss, with "nobility. Unaware of having eliminated savage life", it seeks to appease the "nostalgic cannibalism of history" with mere shadows preserved with great care in museums and libraries.

One could ask at this point, as to what is the nature and significance of the survival of tribal life in India? Is that survival in any way different from what survives of tribal life in the Americas? Or, is it the case that what survives of tribal life in India is also no more than a shadow of what had once been full and truly complete unto itself.

It is significant to note that in India, the tribal situation is marked by two paradoxical facts: the absence of neat demarcations of the tribal as a homogenous social-cultural category, and the significant magnitude of what is accepted as comprising tribal reality. No one can demarcate a clear divide between the tribal and the non-tribal in India. The intensely fluid nature of boundaries between the tribal and the non-tribal are evident in the insuperable difficulty in arriving at a clear anthropological definition of a tribal in India, be that in terms of ethnicity, race, language, social forms or livehood modes.

Remarkably, the Constitution provides for the notification of certain communities as tribal. The notification is on the basis of a varied mix of ethnic, social, linguistic and economic criteria. Hence the prevalent usage as also the only available working definition of a tribal in India: Scheduled Tribes. It would truly be impossible for anyone to say that all the diverse communities listed as Scheduled Tribes conform to the notion of a tribal in its classical sense. At the same time, it would be impossible for anyone to say that all communities that can primarily be regarded as tribal are included in the schedule of Tribes. And yet, for all practical purposes, be it legislation, social-political intervention, collation of data or social theory, the schedule of tribe notified by the Government is the only meaningful referent. Almost every thirteenth Indian is a tribal. Social magnitudes and their persistence as distinct entities over long durations are of immense significance. For they suggest, in however diffused and indirect ways, the structure of cognition and judgment by which a civilisation seeks or could seek to orient itself. The sheer magnitude of tribal survival in India directs attention towards ways of reckoning and engaging with differences that are strikingly unlike the modern historical process.

The past of tribals in India bristles with cruel inflictions. For thousands of years tribal communities have been pushed steadily deeper into the hinterland of remote hills and forests. Vast stretches of land, upon which they had lived their lives, worshipped their deities and nourished their own dreams, have been lost to them. But with all that it remains a past of interaction, utterly unlike the modern past of tribal extinction.

Tribal presence in regions that are predominantly tribal signifies a distinctly different historic quality of tribal-nontribal interaction. Such regions constitute what could be termed tribal contiguities. Within tribal contiguities, choices available to tribal communities for working out their own equations between man and Nature have not been entirely foreclosed in favour of a more advanced mode of livelihood. True, powerful non-tribal rulers did seek to control over tribal contiguities. But pre-modern conquest could never exact more than a nominal annual tribute. The divide in these regions between resistance and restraint, submission and defiance was always somewhat fluid.

The tribal presence within tribal contiguities and its fragmented survival in the midst of non-tribal life may seem at first sight to be far removed and unconnected with each other. But a deep and complex relationship subsists between them. For they together define the place and possibility for tribal life and self-sense in the civilisational matrix of India. Consider in this context the rise to political pre-eminence of the tribal kingdom of Garha in central India during the Sixteenth Century. The stark simplicity of the explanation given by the Abul Fazal, the grand Mughal chronicler, for the rise of Garha invokes rhythms distinctly tribal. For a very long time, records Abul Fazal, rulers of Garha had commanded "reverence" in the region. Yet, they remained powerless until mid Fifteenth Century to translate this "reverence" into political control. Implicit in this fact is the resilience of the distance between reverence and the ability to garner a disproportionately large share of the local surplus.

To this day something of that sense and reality remains alive and vivid in the everyday rhythms of living. Unfettered access to nature furnishes the vital clue to the manifest capacity of tribal cohesions to survive as a distinct entity, despite a long and not always peaceful history of interaction with powerful centres of political authority. Definitive shifts in the relationship between tribal communities and political power began with the consolidation of the modern colonial state in the mid-nineteenth century. As the effective reach of the modern state extended deeper into the hinterland, access to nature came to be progressively restricted.

Choices available to communities even in the remotest parts came to be ever more rigorously foreclosed in favour of the requirements of the state and the world market. Land revenue settlements initiated the process of appropriating vast stretches of tribal lands as "reserved forests" and "government lands". In the tribal contiguity people have lived on a combination of gathering forest produce, grazing, craft skills and shifting or intermittent cultivation. The idea of personal property has been very weak. It is the idea of usage, which defined access to the livelihood resource of the locality of the region.

Tribals in Transition

The modern faith stems from an axiomatic certainty of immense consequence. The grand certainty is that the continually enhanced human capacity to reshape the material world is an unfailing assurance of human liberation and freedom. Progress is the sovereign quest of modern civilisation as also its cardinal referent for meaning and significance. Hence the perception that tribal cohesions represent the survival of archaic social formations which the ever expanding reach of the modern historical process would in time transform and completely recast.

And true enough, the power to reshape the material world has linked and unified the most distant corners of the earth. But for communities and rhythms of life, towards which words like tribe direct our attention, modern unification has meant a virtual half-life on the very margins of modern life and discourse. Consider in this context the intellectual and cultural lineage of the discipline of Ethnology. Its origin and orientation are unmistakably modern. Its mission is to understand and make sense of social facts and forms of thought that clearly do not belong to the modern universe. Levi-Strauss sensed in ethnology a belated sence of remorse. As an intellectual artifact it is inherently ambiguous. It seeks remembrance for facts and forms, which it knows, are marked out for extinction by the very mode of doing and thinking from which ethnology arises. Recognition of definitive difference constitutes as it were its formative substance. And all the while, it knows, that this difference has at best a bleak future in the modern world. In its rare moments of repose modern thought invests rhythms of living forsaken by history, in the words of Levi-Strauss, with "nobility. Unaware of having eliminated savage life", it seeks to appease the "nostalgic cannibalism of history" with mere shadows preserved with great care in museums and libraries.

One could ask at this point, as to what is the nature and significance of the survival of tribal life in India? Is that survival in any way different from what survives of tribal life in the Americas? Or, is it the case that what survives of tribal life in India is also no more than a shadow of what had once been full and truly complete unto itself.

It is significant to note that in India, the tribal situation is marked by two paradoxical facts: the absence of neat demarcations of the tribal as a homogenous social-cultural category, and the significant magnitude of what is accepted as comprising tribal reality. No one can demarcate a clear divide between the tribal and the non-tribal in India. The intensely fluid nature of boundaries between the tribal and the non-tribal are evident in the insuperable difficulty in arriving at a clear anthropological definition of a tribal in India, be that in terms of ethnicity, race, language, social forms or livehood modes.

Remarkably, the Constitution provides for the notification of certain communities as tribal. The notification is on the basis of a varied mix of ethnic, social, linguistic and economic criteria. Hence the prevalent usage as also the only available working definition of a tribal in India: Scheduled Tribes. It would truly be impossible for anyone to say that all the diverse communities listed as Scheduled Tribes conform to the notion of a tribal in its classical sense. At the same time, it would be impossible for anyone to say that all communities that can primarily be regarded as tribal are included in the schedule of Tribes. And yet, for all practical purposes, be it legislation, social-political intervention, collation of data or social theory, the schedule of tribe notified by the Government is the only meaningful referent.

Almost every thirteenth Indian is a tribal. Social magnitudes and their persistence as distinct entities over long durations are of immense significance. For they suggest, in however diffused and indirect ways, the structure of cognition and judgment by which a civilisation seeks or could seek to orient itself. The sheer magnitude of tribal survival in India directs attention towards ways of reckoning and engaging with differences that are strikingly unlike the modern historical process.

The past of tribals in India bristles with cruel inflictions. For thousands of years tribal communities have been pushed steadily deeper into the hinterland of remote hills and forests. Vast stretches of land, upon which they had lived their lives, worshipped their deities and nourished their own dreams, have been lost to them. But with all that it remains a past of interaction, utterly unlike the modern past of tribal extinction.

Tribal presence in regions that are predominantly tribal signifies a distinctly different historic quality of tribal-nontribal interaction. Such regions constitute what could be termed tribal contiguities.

Within tribal contiguities, choices available to tribal communities for working out their own equations between man and Nature have not been entirely foreclosed in favour of a more advanced mode of livelihood. True, powerful non-tribal rulers did seek to control over tribal contiguities. But pre-modern conquest could never exact more than a nominal annual tribute. The divide in these regions between resistance and restraint, submission and defiance was always somewhat fluid.

The tribal presence within tribal contiguities and its fragmented survival in the midst of non-tribal life may seem at first sight to be far removed and unconnected with each other. But a deep and complex relationship subsists between them. For they together define the place and possibility for tribal life and self-sense in the civilisational matrix of India.

Consider in this context the rise to political pre-eminence of the tribal kingdom of Garha in central India during the Sixteenth Century. The stark simplicity of the explanation given by the Abul Fazal, the grand Mughal chronicler, for the rise of Garha invokes rhythms distinctly tribal. For a very long time, records Abul Fazal, rulers of Garha had commanded "reverence" in the region. Yet, they remained powerless until mid Fifteenth Century to translate this "reverence" into political control. Implicit in this fact is the resilience of the distance between reverence and the ability to garner a disproportionately large share of the local surplus.

To this day something of that sense and reality remains alive and vivid in the everyday rhythms of living. Unfettered access to nature furnishes the vital clue to the manifest capacity of tribal cohesions to survive as a distinct entity, despite a long and not always peaceful history of interaction with powerful centres of political authority. Definitive shifts in the relationship between tribal communities and political power began with the consolidation of the modern colonial state in the mid-nineteenth century. As the effective reach of the modern state extended deeper into the hinterland, access to nature came to be progressively restricted.

Choices available to communities even in the remotest parts came to be ever more rigorously foreclosed in favour of the requirements of the state and the world market. Land revenue settlements initiated the process of appropriating vast stretches of tribal lands as "reserved forests" and "government lands". In the tribal contiguity people have lived on a combination of gathering forest produce, grazing, craft skills and shifting or intermittent cultivation. The idea of personal property has been very weak. It is the idea of usage, which defined access to the livelihood resource of the locality of the region.

REFERENCES

Bhowmick, P.K. (1975), "Essential Primary Considerations for Rehabilitation Schemes," *Vanyajati,* October, 1975.

Elwin, Verrier (1964), *A Philosophy for NEFA*, Shillong.

Reddy, G.P. (1977), 'Introducing Agriculture in a Tribal Community:

The Case of the Chenchus", *Proceedings of the Seminar on Integrated Tribal Development Plans*, National Institute of Community Development, Hyderabad.

Tripathy, B. (1971), *A Portrait of Population, Orissa*. Census of India, 1971, Series, 16. Orissa Government Press, Cuttack.

Vidyarthi, L.P. (1975), "Strategy for Tribal Development in India", *Proceedings of the Seminar on Tribal Development*, Bhubaneswar.

8

SOCIOLINGUSTICS AND ANTHROPOLOGY: STRUCTURAL ANALYSIS

> If an American had uttered Winston Churchill's famous line. 'Give us the tools and we will finish the job,' it would have come out, 'Donate the implements and we shall finalize the solution of the matter.'
>
> —*Lord Conesford, M.P.*

Linguistics occupies a special place among the social sciences, to whose ranks it unquestionably belongs. It is not merely a social science like the others, but, rather, the one in which by far the greatest progress has been made. It is probably the only one which can truly claim to be a science and which has achieved both the formulation of an empirical method and an understanding of the nature of the data submitted to its analysis. This privileged position carries with it several obligations. The linguist will often find scientists from related but different disciplines drawing inspiration from his example and trying to follow his lead. *Noblesse oblige*. A linguistic journal like *Word* cannot confine itself to the illustration of strictly linguistic theories and points of view. It must also welcome psychologists, sociologists, and anthropologists eager to learn from modern linguistics the road which leads to the empirical knowledge of social phenomena.

Notably, ever since the work of Schrader it has been unnecessary to demonstrate the assistance which linguistics can render to the anthropologist in the study of kinship. It was a linguist and a philologist (Schrader and Rose) who showed the improbability of the hypothesis of matrilineal survivals in the family in antiquity, to which so many anthropologists still clung at that time. The linguist provides the anthropologist with etymologies which permit him to establish between certain kinship terms relationships that were not immediately apparent. The anthropologist, on the other hand, can bring to the attention of the linguist customs, prescriptions, and prohibitions that help him to understand the persistence of certain features of language or the instability of terms or groups of terms. At a meeting of the Linguistic Circle of New York, Julien Bonfante once illustrated this point of view by reviewing the etymology of the word for uncle in several Romance languages. The Greek *theios* corresponds in Italian, Spanish, and Portuguese to *zio* and *tio*; and he added that in certain regions of Italy the uncle is called *barba*. The "beard," the "divine" uncle — what a wealth of suggestions for the anthropologist! The investigations of the late A.M. Hocart into the religious character of the avuncular relationship and "theft of the sacrifice" by the maternal kinsmen immediately come to mind. Whatever interpretation is given to the data collected by Hocart (and his own interpretation is not entirely satisfactory), there is no doubt that the linguist contributes to the solution of the problem by revealing the tenacious survival in contemporary vocabulary of relationships which have long since disappeared. At the same time, the anthropologist explains to the linguist the bases of etymology and confirms its validity. Paul K. Benedict, in examining, as a linguist, the kinship systems of South East Asia, was able to make an important contribution to the anthropology of the family in that area.

Remarkably, linguists and anthropologists follow their own paths independently as a general practice. They halt , no doubt, from time to time to communicate to one another certain of their findings; these findings, however, derive from different operations, and no effort is made to enable one group to benefit from the technical and methodological advances of the other. This attitude might have been justified in the era when linguistic research leaned most heavily on historical analysis. In relation to the anthropological research conducted during the same period, the difference was one of degree rather than of kind.

The linguists employed a more rigorous method, and their findings were established on more solid grounds; the sociologists could follow their example in renouncing consideration of the spatial distribution of contemporary types as a basis for their classifications. But, after all, anthropology more so sociology were looking to linguistics only for insights; nothing foretold a revelation.

Notably, the advent of structural linguistics completely changed this situation. Not only did it renew linguistic perspectives; a transformation of this magnitude is not limited to a single discipline. Structural linguistics will certainly play the same renovating role with respect to the social sciences that nuclear physics, for example, has played for the physical sciences. In what does this revolution consist, as we try to assess its broadest implications? N. Troubetzkoy, the illustrious founder of structural linguistics, himself furnished the answer to this question. In one programmatic statement, he reduced the structural method to four basic operations. First, structural linguistics shifts from the study of *conscious linguistic* phenomena to study of their *unconscious* infrastructure; second, it does not treat *terms* as independent entities, taking instead as its - basis of analysis the *relations* between terms; third, it introduces the concept of *system* - "Modern phonemics does not merely proclaim that phonemes are always part of a system; it *shows* concrete phonemic systems and elucidates their structure" finally, structural linguistics aims at discovering *general laws,* either by induction "or . . . by logical deduction, which would give them an absolute character."

Thus, for the first time, a social science is able to formulate necessary relationships. This is the meaning of Troubetzkoy's last point, while the preceding rules show how linguistics must proceed in order to attain this end. It is not for us to show that Troubetzkoy's claims are justified. The vast majority of modern linguists seem sufficiently agreed on this point. But when an event of this importance takes place in one of the sciences of man, it is not only permissible for, but required of, representatives of related disciplines immediately to examine its consequences and its possible application to phenomena of another order.

New perspectives then open up. We are no longer dealing with an occasional collaboration where the linguist and the anthropologist, each working by himself, occasionally communicate those findings which each thinks may interest the other. In the study of kinship problems (and, no doubt, the study of other problems as well), the anthropologist finds himself in a situation which formally resembles that of the structural linguist. Like phonemes, kinship terms are elements of meaning; like phonemes, they acquire meaning only if they are integrated into systems.

"Kinship systems," Eke "phonemic systems," are built by the mind on the level of unconscious thought. Finally, the recurrence of kinship patterns, marriage rules, similar prescribed attitudes between certain types of relatives, and so forth, in scattered regions of the globe and in fundamentally different societies, leads us to believe that, in the case of kinship as well as linguistics, the observable phenomena result from the action of laws which are general but implicit. The problem can therefore be formulated as follows: Although they belong to *another order of reality*, kinship phenomena are *of the same type* as linguistic phenomena.

The study of kinship problems is today broached in the same terms and seems to be in the throes of the same difficulties as was linguistics on the eve of the structuralist revolution. There is a striking analogy between certain attempts by Rivers and the old linguistics, which sought its explanatory principles first of all in history. In both cases, it is solely (or almost solely) diachronic analysis which must account for synchronic phenomena. Troubetzkoy, comparing structural linguistics and the old linguistics, defines structural linguistics as a "systematic structuralism and universalism," which he contrasts with the individualism and "atomism" of former schools. And when he considers diachronic analysis, his perspective is a profoundly modified one: "The evolution of a phonemic system at any given moment is directed by the *tendency toward a goal. ...* This evolution thus has a direction, an internal logic, which historical phonemics is called upon to elucidate." The "individualistic" and "atomistic" interpretation, founded exclusively on historical contingency, which is criticised by Troubetzkoy and Jakobson, is actually the same as that which is generally applied to kinship problems. Each detail of terminology and each special marriage rule is associated with a specific custom as either its consequence or its survival. We thus meet with a chaos of discontinuity. No one asks how kinship systems, regarded as synchronic wholes, could be the arbitrary product of a convergence of several heterogeneous institutions (most of which are hypothetical), yet nevertheless function with some sort of regularity and effectiveness.

Significantly, a preliminary difficulty impedes the transposition of the phonemic method to the anthropological study of primitive peoples. The superficial analogy between phonemic systems and kinship systems is so strong that it immediately sets us on the wrong track. It is incorrect to equate kinship terms and linguistic phonemes from the viewpoint of their formal treatment. We know that to obtain a structural law the linguist analyses phonemes into "distinctive features," which he can then group into one or several "pairs of oppositions." Following an analogous method, the anthropologist might be tempted to break down analytically the kinship terms of any given system into their components. In our own kinship system, for instance, the term *father* has positive connotations with respect to sex, relative age, and generation; but it has a zero value on the dimension of collaterality, and it cannot express an affinal relationship. Thus, for each system, one might ask what relationships are expressed and, for each term of the system, what connotation - positive or negative - it carries regarding each of the following relationships: generation, collaterality, sex, relative age, affinity, etc. It is at this "micro-sociological" level that one might hope to discover the most general structural laws, just as the linguist discovers his at the infraphonemic level or the physicist at the infra-molecular or atomic level.

Surprising again, a threefold objection immediately arises. A truly scientific analysis must be real, simplifying, and explanatory. Thus the distinctive features which are the product of phonemic analysis have an objective existence from three points of view: psychological, physiological, and even physical; they are fewer in number than the phonemes which result from their combination; and, finally, they allow us to understand and reconstruct the system. Nothing of the kind would emerge from the preceding hypothesis. The treatment of kinship terms which we have just sketched is analytical in appearance only; for, actually, the result is more abstract than the principle; instead of moving toward the concrete, one moves away from it, and the definitive system - if system there is - is only conceptual. Secondly, Davis and Warner's experiment proves that the system achieved through this procedure is infinitely more complex and more difficult to interpret than the empirical data. Finally, the hypothesis has no explanatory value; that is, it does not lead to an understanding of the nature of the system and still less to a reconstruction of its origins.

A too literal adherence to linguistic method actually betrays its very essence. Kinship terms not only have a sociological existence; they are also elements of speech. In our haste to apply the methods of linguistic analysis, we must not forget that, as a part of vocabulary, kinship terms must be treated with linguistic methods in direct and not analogous fashion.

Linguistics teaches us precisely that structural analysis cannot be applied to words directly, but only to words previously broken down into phonemes. *There are no necessary relationships at the vocabulary level*. This applies to all vocabulary elements, including kinship terms. Since this applies to linguistics, it ought to apply *ipso facto* to the sociology of language. An attempt like the one whose possibility we are now discussing would thus consist in extending the method of structural linguistics while ignoring its basic requirements.

Kroeber prophetically foresaw this difficulty in an article written many years ago. And if, at that time, he concluded that a structural analysis of kinship terminology was impossible, we must remember that linguistics itself was then restricted to phonetic, psychological, and historical analysis. While it is true that the social sciences must share the limitations of linguistics, they can also benefit from its progress. Nor should we overlook the profound differences between the phonemic chart of a language and the chart of kinship terms of a society. In the first instance there can be no question as to function; we all know that language serves as a means of communication. On the other hand, what the linguist did not know and what structural linguistics alone has allowed him to discover is the way in which language achieves this end. The function was obvious; the system remained unknown. In this respect, the anthropologist finds himself in the opposite situation.

We should at least recognise the special problems raised by the sociology of vocabulary and the ambiguous character of the relations between its methods and those of linguistics. For this reason it would be preferable to limit the discussion to a case where the analogy can be clearly established. Fortunately, we have just such a case available.

What is generally called a "kinship system" comprises two quite different orders of reality. First, there are terms through which various kinds of family relationships are expressed. But kinship is not expressed solely through nomenclature. The individuals or classes of individuals who employ these terms feel (or do not feel, as the case may be) bound by prescribed behaviour in their relations with one another, such as respect or familiarity, rights or obligations, and affection or hostility.

Thus, along with what we propose to call the *system of terminology* (which, strictly speaking, constitutes the vocabulary system), there is another system, both psychological and social in nature, which we shall call the *system of attitudes.* Although it is true that the study of systems of terminology places us in a situation analogous, but opposite, to the situation in which we are dealing with phonemic systems, this difficulty is "inversed," as it were, when we examine systems of attitudes. We can guess at the role played by systems of attitudes, that is, to insure group cohesion and equilibrium, but we do not understand the nature of the interconnections between the various attitudes, nor do we perceive their necessity. In other words, as in the case of language, we know their function, but the system is unknown.

Thus we find a profound difference between the *system of terminology* and the *system of attitudes,* and we have to disagree with A.R. Radcliffe-Brown if he really believed, as has been said of him, that attitudes are nothing but the expression or transposition of terms on the affective level. The last few years have provided numerous examples of groups whose chart of kinship terms does not accurately reflect family attitudes, and vice versa. It would be incorrect to assume that the kinship system constitutes the principal means of regulating interpersonal relationships in all societies. Even in societies where the kinship system does function as such, it does not fulfil that role everywhere to the same extent. Furthermore, it is always necessary to distinguish between two types of attitudes: first, the diffuse, uncrystallised, and non-institutionalised attitudes, which we may consider as the reflection or transposition of the terminology on the psychological level; and second, along with, or in addition to, the preceding ones, those attitudes which are stylised, prescribed, and sanctioned by taboos or privileges and expressed through a fixed ritual.

These attitudes, far from automatically reflecting the nomenclature, often appear as secondary elaborations, which serve to resolve the contradictions and overcome the deficiencies inherent in the terminological system. This synthetic character is strikingly apparent among the Wik Munkan of Australia. In this group, joking privileges sanction a contradiction between the kinship relations which link two unmarried men and the theoretical relationship which must be assumed to exist between them in order to account for their later marriages to two women who do not stand themselves in the corresponding relationship.

There is a contradiction between two possible systems of nomenclature, and the emphasis placed on attitudes represents an attempt to integrate or transcend this contradiction. We can easily agree with Radcliffe-Brown and assert the existence of real relations of interdependence between the terminology and the rest of the system. Some of his critics made the mistake of inferring from the absence of a rigorous parallelism between attitudes and nomenclature, that the two systems were mutually independent. But this relationship of interdependence does not imply a one-to-one correlation. The system of attitudes constitutes, rather, a dynamic integration of the system of terminology.

Structure and Dialectics

From Lang to Malinowski, through Durkheim, Lévy-

Bruhl, and van der Leeuw, sociologists and anthropologists who were interested in the interrelations between myth and ritual have considered them as mutually redundant. Some of these thinkers see in each myth the ideological projection of a rite, the purpose of the myth being to provide a foundation for the rite. Others reverse the relationship and regard ritual as a kind of dramatised illustration of the myth. Regardless of whether the myth or the ritual is the original, they replicate each other; the myth exists on the conceptual level and the ritual on the level of action. In both cases, one assumes an orderly correspondence between the two, in other words, a homology. Curiously enough, this homology is demonstrable in only a small number of cases. It remains to be seen why all myths do not correspond to rites and vice versa, and most important, why there should be such a curious replication in the first place.

Social Structure

It is obvious that the term "social structure" needs first to be defined and that some explanation should be given of the difference which helps to distinguish studies in social structure from the unlimited field of descriptions, analyses, and theories dealing with social relations at large, which merge with the whole scope of social anthropology. This is all the more necessary, since some of those who have contributed toward setting apart social structure as a special field of anthropological studies conceived the former in many different manners and even sometimes, so it seems, came to nurture grave doubts as to the validity of their enterprise. For instance, Kroeber writes in the second edition of his *Anthropology:*

> "Structure" appears to be just a yielding to a word that has perfectly good meaning but suddenly becomes fashionably attractive for a decade or so - like

> "streamlining" - and during its vogue tends to be applied indiscriminately because of the pleasurable connotations of its sound. Of course a typical personality can be viewed as having a structure. But so can a physiology, any organism, all societies and all cultures, crystals, machines - in fact everything that is not wholly amorphous has a structure. So what "structure" adds to the meaning of our phrase seems to be nothing, except to provoke a degree of pleasant puzzlement.'

Although this passage concerns more particularly the notion of "basic personality structure," it has devastating implications as regards the generalised use of the notion of structure in anthropology.

Another reason makes a definition of social structure compulsory: From the structuralist point of view which one has to adopt if only to give the problem its meaning, it would be hopeless to try to reach a valid definition of social structure on an inductive basis, by abstracting common elements from the uses and definitions current among all the scholars who claim to have made "social structure" the object of their studies. If these concepts have a meaning at all, they mean, first, that the notion of structure has a structure. This we shall try to outline from the beginning as a precaution against letting ourselves be submerged by a tedious inventory of books and papers dealing with social relations, the mere listing of which would more than exhaust the limited space at our disposal. At a further stage we will have to see how far and in what directions the term "social structure," as used by the different authors, departs from our definition.

The term "social structure" has nothing to do with empirical reality but with models which are built up after it. This should help one to clarify difference between two concepts which are so close to each that they have often been confused, namely, those of *social structure* and of *social relations.* It will be enough to state at this social relations consist of the raw materials out of which the models making up the social structure are built, while social structure can, by no means, be reduced to the ensemble of the social relations to be described in a given society.

Therefore, social structure cannot claim a field of its own among others in the social studies. It is rather a method to be applied to any kind of social studies, similar to the structural analysis current in other disciplines. The question then becomes that of ascertaining what kind of model deserves the name "structure." This is not an anthropological question, but one which belongs to the methodology of science in general. Keeping this in mind, we can say that a structure consists of a model meeting with several requirements.

First, the structure exhibits the characteristics of a system. It is made up of several elements, none of which can undergo a change without effecting changes in all the other elements.

Second, for any given model there should be a possibility of ordering a series of transformations resulting in a group of models of the same type.

Third, the above properties make it possible to predict how the model will react if one or more of its elements are submitted to certain modifications.

Finally, the model should be constituted so as to make immediately intelligible all the observed facts.

These being the requirements for any model with

structural value, several consequences follow. These, however, do not pertain to the definition of structure, but have to do with the chief properties exhibited and problems raised by structural analysis when contemplated in the social and other fields.

Further utmost care should be taken to distinguish between the observational and the experimental levels. To observe facts and elaborate methodological devices which permit the construction of models out of these facts is not at all the same thing as to experiment on the models. By "experimenting on models," we mean the set of procedures aiming at ascertaining how a given model will react when subjected to change and at comparing models of the same or different types.

This distinction is all the more necessary, since many discussions on social structure revolve around the apparent contradiction between the concreteness and individuality of ethnological data and the abstract and formal character generally exhibited by structural studies. This contradiction, disappears as one comes to realise that these features belong to two entirely different levels, or rather to two stages of the same process. On the observational level, in the main one could almost say the only rule is that all the facts should be carefully observed and described, without allowing any theoretical preconception to decide whether some are more important than others.

This rule together with its corollaries has been explicitly formulated by K. Goldstein in relation to psycho-physiological studies, and it may be considered valid for any kind of structural analysis. Its immediate consequence is that, far from being contradictory, there is a direct relationship between the detail and concreteness of ethnographical description and the validity and generality of the model which is constructed after it. For, though many models may be used as convenient devices to describe and explain the phenomena, it is obvious that the best model will always be that which is *true,* that is, the simplest possible model which, while being derived exclusively from the facts under consideration, also makes it possible to account for all of them.

Again a second distinction has to do with the conscious or unconscious character of the models. In the history of structural thought, Boas may be credited with having introduced this distinction. He made clear that a category of facts can more easily yield to structural analysis when the social group in which it is manifested has not elaborated a conscious model to interpret or justify it. Some readers may be surprised to find Boas' name quoted in connection with structural theory, since he has often been described as one of the main obstacles in its path. But this writer has tried to demonstrate that Boas' shortcomings in matters of structural studies did not lie in his failure to understand their importance and significance, which he did, as a matter of fact, in the most prophetic way.

They rather resulted from the fact that he imposed on structural studies conditions of validity, some of which will remain forever part of their methodology, while some others are so exacting and impossible to meet that they would have withered scientific development in any field. A structural model may be conscious or unconscious without this difference affecting its nature. It can only be said that when the structure of a certain type of phenomena does not lie at a great depth, it is more likely that some kind of model, standing as a screen to hide it, will exist in the collective consciousness.

For conscious models, which are usually known as "norms," are by definition very poor ones, since they are not intended to explain the phenomena but to perpetuate them. Therefore, structural analysis is confronted with a strange paradox well known to the linguist, that is: the more obvious structural organisation is, the more difficult it becomes to reach it because of the inaccurate conscious models lying across the path which leads to it. From the point of view of the degree of consciousness, the anthropologist is confronted with two kinds of situations. He may have to construct a model from phenomena the systematic character of which has evoked no awareness on the part of the culture; this is the kind of simpler situation referred to by Boas as providing the easiest ground for anthropological research. Or else the anthropologist will be dealing on the one hand with raw phenomena and on the other with the models already constructed by the culture to interpret the former. Though it is likely that, for the reasons stated above, these models will prove unsatisfactory, it is by no means necessary that this should always be the case. As a matter of fact, many "primitive" cultures have built models of their marriage regulations which are much more to the point than models built by professional anthropologists Thus one cannot dispense with studying a culture's "home-made" models for two reasons. First, these models might prove to be accurate or, at least, to provide some insight into the structure of the phenomena; after all, each culture has its own theoreticians whose contributions deserve the same attention as that which the anthropologist gives to colleagues. And, second, even if the models are biased or erroneous, the very bias and type of error are a part of the facts under study and probably rank among the most significant ones. But even when taking into consideration these culturally produced models, the anthropologist does not forget — as he has sometimes been accused of doing - that the cultural norms are not of themselves structures. Rather, they furnish an important contribution to an understanding of the structures, either as factual documents or as theoretical contributions similar to those of the anthropologist himself.

Remarkably, this point has been given great attention by the French sociological school. Durkheim and Mauss, for instance, have always taken care to substitute, as a starting point for the survey of native categories of thought, the conscious representations prevailing among the natives themselves for those stemming from the anthropologist's own culture. This was undoubtedly an important step, which, nevertheless, fell short of its goal because these authors were not sufficiently aware that native conscious representations, important as they are, may be just as remote from the unconscious reality as any other.

[Acknowledgment: This chapter is develop on the basis of Claude Lavi-Strauss. We owe a deep sense of gratitude to the great scholar for subscribing his views. —*Ed.*]

9

ETHICS IN ANTHROPOLOGY

> "The only way to get rid of responsibilities is to discharge them".
>
> —*Walter S. Robertson*

A famous adage goes "morality is simply the attitude we adopt toward people whom we personally dislike." (Oscar Wilde). Many anthropologists perceive ethics as an abstract and, on occasion, intimidating set of injunctions. Discussions of moral principles—such as autonomy, nonmaleficence, beneficence, and justice—seem to have little relation to our daily activities as researchers, teachers, students, and practitioners.

Several anthropologists were moved to enter the discipline because of a strong concern for the peoples of the world. During their fieldwork, most have developed a strong empathy for the peoples they have studied and have felt a sense of personal responsibility for their welfare. Hence, when they use, hurt, or endanger others, it is usually not because of a vicious disposition, but because they are under strong pressures, some of which are conflicting or difficult to reconcile, and they may then drift into an expedient course of action that proves unwise.

Significantly, the cross-pressures of modern fieldwork are severe, and they can easily induce an investigator to treat the host people as "subjects," rather than as fellow human beings whose autonomy must be respected. While completing a graduate degree, or submitting a prompt report to an employer or client, or resolving an intense emotional relationship, we may neglect to consider other factors in the situation or the consequences our actions will have for others. Convictions, leading presumably to the abstract and universal benefit of humanity, can be used to justify the violation of agreements entered into with good faith on both sides. Awareness that others are acting exploitatively or immorally can seductively encourage us to adopt a similar orientation. In the field especially, situations may be so complex, involve so many parties and so much factionalism, that it becomes difficult to decide what must be done.

We do not wish to make ethics seem merely a matter of isolated choices in crucial situations. Much of our lives proceeds undramatically, and often our decisions are almost imperceptible, so that only with hindsight are we aware that our course of action had consequences that we had not foreseen and now regret. To improve the ethical adequacy of anthropological practice, we must consider not only exceptional cases but everyday decisions, and reflect not only upon the conduct of others but also upon our own actions.

In spite of difficulties in writing a code specific enough to use as a mechanism of social control, a code of ethics can help improve anthropological practice. When it is conceived as a way of reflecting upon our own practices and attempting to improve them, as well as a method for regulating behavior, a code can heighten sensitivity to professional conduct. In this twofold approach, a code is concerned with aspirations as well as avoidances; it represents our desire and attempt to respect the rights of others, fulfill obligations, avoid harm, and augment benefits to those we interact with as anthropologists. Such a code is less a set of categorical prohibitions engraved in stone, than a series of aspirations, admonitions, and injunctions to be considered, discussed, and periodically altered by the community of anthropologists.

Further, case studies offer another way to heighten sensitivity and improve anthropological practice. An ethical dilemma may be difficult to recognize when encountered; "practical" decisions frequently turn out to have ethical ramifications. Reading and thinking about situations faced by other anthropologists can help us.

From its emergence as a distinct discipline, anthropology has been oriented toward ethics and social policy. Edward B. Tylor concluded his survey of human culture with the remark that "the science of culture is essentially a reformer's science" (1958[1871]:539). A.R. Radcliffe-Brown would claim that he was moved to initiate his studies of simpler peoples on the advice of the celebrated Russian anarchist, Prince Peter Kropotkin, for whom such peoples manifested a system of organization which could prove an exemplar in a world dominated by autocracy and nationalism (Srinivas 1958:xviii). In the period pre-World War I, this ideal of anthropology as an ethical calling above the petty rivalries of nationalism inspired Franz Boas to moral outrage when he suspected that the disciplinary role had been used to cloak espionage (1919:797).

Until World War II, much of the anthropological literature on "morals" or "ethics" was directed from ethnology toward philosophy. The latter discipline was dominated by linguistic formalism in the service of a positivistic worldview, and philosophical ethics inquired as to the possible meanings of propositions such as "X is good" (MacIntyre 1981:Chapter 2). In this situation, it was a helpful contribution for MacBeath (1952) to use anthropological data to exhibit the varieties of ethical systems in natural societies. Brandt, a professional philosopher, studied Hopi ethics (1954), while Ladd studied Navajo ethics (1957), and Abraham Edel, the philosopher, collaborated with May Edel, the anthropologist, in interdisciplinary efforts (1955, 1959). Bidney, a professor of both anthropology and philosophy, labored to clarify the notion of "value" (1962).

No exaggeration, "ethics" were topics of serious concern among fieldworking anthropologists, the central issues were relativism and intervention. Since the history of relativism within anthropology has recently been neatly summarized by Hatch (1983), there is little need for me to repeat the review, except to note that the issue did and does provoke considerable discussion among professional philosophers (e.g., Krausz and Meiland 1982; Wellman 1963). It is sufficient to note the exchanges between the humanistic student of civilization, Redfield (1953), and the "orthodox" defender of cultural relativism, Herskovits (1973). On "intervention" the issue was whether or not, or how, to assist the people with whom one was involved as a fieldworker.

Typically, such peoples were subjects of a Western colonial power, whose administration an anthropologist might hope to influence. For many fieldworkers the problem was intensified because of the notion that each culture was an integrated whole whose harmony might be damaged by casual intervention. Likewise, many felt constrained by the methodological ideal of the natural scientist, who was intrinsically detached from the objects of study. These concerns were rendered nugatory by the rise of Nazism, fascism, and totalitarianism, regimes which conquered, enslaved, or massacred many peoples. In the ensuing war, anthropologists found themselves encouraged to serve in a variety of capacities. Faced with the threats of fascism and Nazism, most did so with great willingness, and, in this context, "ethics" became defined as the willingness to sacrifice professional career, or even life and limb, in the cause of "the Free World," of which the U.S. appeared to be the military and spiritual leader.

Because of their cross-cultural training, a number of anthropologists were recruited into military intelligence. others were commissioned as officers. Some were also involved in the complex processes after World War II, which involved peoples who had been enslaved, decimated, or displaced and were now liberated from brutal regimes. In accepting these roles, anthropologists could regard their conduct as simply the logical extension of their earlier benevolent roles acting as cultural broker or mediator, assisting peoples with simpler technology in their encounter with the civilized world.

In the post World War II, a polar fission of political worldviews erupted within the discipline. Federal agencies and private foundations were encouraging the growth of anthropology to match the responsibilities that the U.S. government now saw itself shouldering. A generation of dedicated and educated young people were studying anthropology and conducting fieldwork in the far comers of the earth. They returned with a sober and disenchanted view; they perceived great misery and continued oppression; projects that were publicly rationalized as benefiting tribal peoples were in fact actually benefiting members or strata of the ruling powers. Most important, the new anthropologists were encountering political rebelliousness guided by a sophisticated elite. Where, in an earlier age, fieldworkers had dealt with nonliterate peoples isolated from modern communications, now they were encountering leaders familiar with the rhetoric of Western political discourse, including its nationalism, populism, and Marxism.

In North America, the witty satire and sage intercultural critique of Vine Deloria, Jr., (Sioux) heralded a new age in which anthropologists were to be called to account by Indian representatives. While he is known among the public for his ridicule of fieldworkers, in collegial communication he urges anthropologists to reflect seriously about the effects of their work and to assume a helpful role in relation to the abundant problems of Indian peoples (1980). Other Native American leaders have unfurled the banner of "Red Power" and provoked a series of dramatic confrontations with federal authorities. These became exciting events for the media but troublesome cases for anthropologists, because it was not clear what was desired by—or desirable for—the larger aggregate of Indian communities.

While the pre-World War II generation of anthropologists had regarded their national military and intelligence services with an ethically neutral (or, in some cases, beneficent) eye, the following generations developed the suspicious and antagonistic view of Third World leaders. From this perspective, employment with these national agencies was a prostitution of valuable professional talents for monies and prestige; it was a betrayal of the peoples whose welfare anthropology had claimed to cherish.

"Ethics" were now defined as a conscientious refusal to accept such monies or employment. Nevertheless, many of the older generation continued to have faith in the difference between a democratic United States and its (past or present) totalitarian rivals (Nazi Germany, Fascist Italy, Imperial Japan, Stalinist Soviet Union). Where one group was impressed with the exploitation of peoples struggling under colonial or imperialist rule, the other was impressed with the miseries under fascist and Bolshevik-Leninist regimes.

By the time that the United States had become militarily involved in the conflict in Southeast Asia, the pendulum had thus swung far in the direction where "ethics" were defined as a refusal to have any dealings with the military side of government, or with any aspect of government that seemed to sustain an imperialistic orientation. While the political rhetoric was heated, the literature dealt with important and difficult issues.

In the revulsion following the Nuremberg trials, there emerged a powerful social movement emphasizing the notion of individual moral responsibility, regardless of the dictates of the officials of the state or of other organized bodies. Correlatively, there emerged the notion of monitoring the conduct of physicians and biomedical researchers, so that they did not abuse or exploit their patients in the name of science or any other ideological principle. The regulatory system thus instituted spread to include any scientific discipline that could be regarded as having "human subjects" who were subjected to procedures that imposed risks, or that might, without their consent, be inflictive of harm. The resultant biomedical literature is now considerable, and while it is diverse and uneven, at its core are essays of depth which illuminate the critical social issues. If there is a weakness to the literature it derives from the predispositions of mainstream U.S. culture, namely its individualism, its reluctance to accept the notion that there may be values more significant than life (brute existence), and its inability to face the dilemmas that ensue when social resources are finite. As this movement (Wulff 1979) gained momentum, anthropological fieldworkers found themselves confronting Institutional Review Boards (IRBs), whose existence was mandated by the federal government as a condition of institutional eligibility for participation in the economy of grants, fellowships, and contracts. Since the relevant commissions had taken no testimony from anthropologists about the moral issues of their research, the regulations were framed to control the activities of biomedical researchers, and so applied but clumsily to the process of fieldwork. Meanwhile, university administrators were using the regulatory system as a device to regulate or even suppress such activities as public opinion polls conducted by student newspapers. The resulting institutional friction generated not only movements of protest but of inquiry and research that have helped to illuminate the ethical issues in anthropological fieldwork (Wax and Cassell 1979).

In this process, "ethics" for anthropologists became redefined as having to do with the nature of interaction between fieldworker and hosts, and, in particular, with such issues as "informed consent" and with whether or not benefit (or harm) might issue from the project (Cassell and Wax 1980). The morality of covert field research remains a key issue; it is noteworthy that this issue could not and cannot arise in many traditional anthropological contexts (e.g., Raymond Firth in Tikopia; Jean Briggs among the Utku of Chantrey Inlet), but it can and does arise when fieldwork is attempted among modern urban populations (Bulmer 1982).

An incidental consequence has been that a number of philosophers have moved from the linguistic analysis of moral statements to an engagement with social policy. Others have reviewed the history of ethical deliberation from a standpoint that is influenced by the sociology and anthropology of knowledge. Particularly outstanding has been the work of Alasdair MacIntyre (1966, 1981), a professional philosopher who has an excellent familiarity with the social sciences.

APPENDIX

SOME PROMINENT ANTHROPOLOGISTS

- John Adair
- Manuel Laranjeira Rodrigues de Areia
- Talal Asad
- Michael Asch
- Timothy Asch
- Nigel Barley
- Christine Barrow
- Fredrik Barth
- Vasily Bartold
- Keith H. Basso
- Daisy Bates
- Ruth Behar
- Stephen Beckerman
- Thomas Belmonte
- Ruth Benedict
- Theodore C. Bestor
- Joao Biehl
- Lewis Binford
- Karen Blu
- Wilhelm Bleek

- Anton Blok
- Franz Boas
- Dmitri Bondarenko
- James Boon
- Robert Borofsky
- Pere Bosch-Gimpera
- Pierre Bourdieu
- Brent Berlin
- Jeremy Boissevain
- Paul Broca
- Hugh Brody
- Peter J. Brown
- Carole Browner
- Sir Peter Buck
- Mauro Campagnoli
- Joseph Campbell
- Edmund Carpenter
- Napoleon Chagnon
- Miguel Chase-Sardi
- Pierre Clastres
- Jean Comaroff
- John Comaroff
- Carleton S. Coon
- Vincent Crapanzano
- Julie Cruickshank
- Frank Hamilton Cushing
- Regna Darnell

- Raymond Dart
- Patrick E. de Josselin de Jong
- Ella Cara Deloria
- Frederica De Laguna
- Raymond J. DeMallie
- Stanley Diamond
- Miguel Diaz-Barriga
- Mary Douglas
- Eugene Dubois
- Sam Dunn
- Émile Durkheim
- Mircea Eliade
- E. E. Evans-Pritchard
- Arturo Escobar
- James D. Faubion
- Raymond Firth
- Henri Th. Fischer
- Raymond D. Fogelson
- Meyer Fortes
- Diane Fossey
- Michel Foucault
- James Frazer
- Morton H. Fried
- Cathirne Fisher
- James Ferguson
- Geri-Ann Galanti
- Linda Garro

- Clifford Geertz
- Alfred Gell
- Ernest Gellner
- Eugenia Georges
- Abhik Ghosh
- Faye Ginsburg
- Max Gluckman
- Maurice Godelier
- Byron Good
- Mary Jo Good
- Jane Goodall
- Robert J Gordon
- Chris Gosden
- David Graeber
- Hilma Granqvist
- J. Patrick Gray
- Carol J. Greenhouse
- Ina M. Greverus
- Marcel Griaule
- Jacob Grimm
- Wilhelm Grimm
- Horatio Hale
- Paul Hammacott
- Peter Hammond
- Michael Harkin
- Michael Harner
- John P. Harrington

- Marvin Harris
- Jacquetta Hawkes
- Cassidy Hendrickson
- Edgar Lee Hewett
- Paul G. Hiebert
- Arthur Maurice Hocart
- Jon Holtzman
- Earnest Hooton
- Ian Hodder
- E. Adamson Hoebel
- Thomas Hokin
- F.Clark Howell
- Aleš Hrdlièka
- Patrick Hunout
- Zora Neale Hurston
- Dell Hymes
- Miyako Inoue (linguistic anthropologist)
- Inger Interlach
- Barbara Rose Johnston
- William Jones (philologist)
- Schuyler ("Skye") Jones
- Sergei Kan
- Alice Kehoe
- Jomo Kenyatta
- David Kertzer
- Anatoly Khazanov
- Richard G. Klein

- Peter Kloos
- Pete Knutson
- André Köbben
- Dorinne K. Kondo
- Andrey Korotayev
- Conrad Kottak
- Grover Krantz
- Charles H. Kraft
- Shepard Krech III
- Kewal Krishan
- Alfred L. Kroeber
- Theodora Kroeber
- Adam Kuper
- Hilda Kuper
- William Labov
- George Lakoff
- Harold E. Lambert
- Louise Lamphere
- Ruth Landes
- Clark S. Larsen
- Bruno Latour
- Edmund Leach
- Murray Leaf
- Louis Leakey
- Mary Leakey
- Richard Leakey
- Richard Borshay Lee

- Claude Lévi-Strauss
- Robert Lowie
- Alan Macfarlane
- Saba Mahmood
- Bronis³aw Malinowski
- George Marcus
- John Alden Mason
- Marcel Mauss
- Phillip McArthur
- Grant McCracken
- David W. McCurdy
- Margaret Mead
- Mervyn Meggitt
- Josef Mengele
- Alfred Métraux
- Nikolay Miklukho-Maklay
- H. Paul Manning
- Emily Martin
- Sidney Mintz
- Ashley Montagu
- James Mooney
- John H. Moore
- Lewis H. Morgan
- Leith Mullings
- Nancy Munn
- George Murdock
- Peter Nabokov

- Laura Nader
- Raoul Naroll
- Curt Nimuendajú
- Erland Nordenskiöld
- Gananath Obeyesekere
- Elinor Ochs
- Gordon Orians
- Emiko Ohnuki-Tierney
- Marvin Opler
- Morris Opler
- Sherry Ortner
- Martin Ottenheimer
- Bruce Parry (television show host)
- Elsie Clews Parsons
- James Peacock
- Glenn Petersen
- Bronislav Pilsudski
- Hortense Powdermaker
- A.H.J. Prins
- Harald E.L. Prins
- James Quesada
- Paul Rabinow
- Wilhelm Radloff
- Rayna Rapp
- Roy Rappaport
- Hans Ras
- Rhoda Reddock

- Alfred Reginald Radcliffe-Brown
- Gerardo Reichel-Dolmatoff
- Kathy Reichs
- Audrey Richards
- W. H. R. Rivers
- Paul Rivet
- Charolette Rogers
- Erich von Rosen
- Lawrence Rosen
- Eric Ross
- Gayle Rubin
- Robert A. Rubinstein
- Chip Royston
- Marshall Sahlins
- Roger Sandall
- Edward Sapir
- Nancy Scheper-Hughes
- Wilhelm Schmidt
- Tobias Schneebaum
- Thayer Scudder
- Elman Service
- Afanasy Shchapov
- Cathy Small
- Jacques Soustelle
- Frank G. Speck
- Melford Spiro
- James Spradley

- Julian Steward
- Pradip Kumar Singh
- Herbert Spencer
- Ann L. Stoler
- Bilinda Straight
- Andrew Strathern
- Marilyn Strathern
- William Sturtevant
- Naqiyah Sultan
- Michael Taussig
- Edward Burnett Tylor
- Colin Turnbull
- Edith Turner
- Terence Turner
- Victor Turner
- Bruce Trigger
- Albert Trouwborst
- Ulla Johansen
- Verrier Elwin
- Christine VanPool
- Karl Verner
- L. P. Vidyarthi
- Max Weber
- Camilla Wedgwood
- Hank Wesselman
- Ben White
- Douglas R. White

- Leslie White
- Tim White
- Neil Whitehead
- Benjamin Whorf
- Unni Wikan
- Clark Wissler
- Eric Wolf
- Sol Worth

GLOSSARY

Acculturation - culture change resulting from contact between cultures. A process of external culture change.

Adaptation - patterns of behavior which enable a culture to cope with its surroundings.

Adjudication - mediation with the ultimate decision being made by an unbiased third party.

Affinal - members of one's kindred who are related through a marital linkage.

Age grade - a social category or status based on an age range.

Age set - a social group defined by those who share the same age status and are a recognizable group.

Aggression - acts or threats designed to cause injury.

Ambilineal - a corporate kin group that traces relationships through either the female or male lines. Also called cognatic descent.

American Anthropological Association (AAA) - the major professional association for anthropologists in the United States.

Animatism - belief in an impersonal and divisible supernatural force or forces, which reside in living or unliving things.

Animism - a belief that natural phenomena such as rocks, trees, thunder, or celestial bodies have life or divinity.

Anthropological linguistics - the branch of anthropology that studies human language. Linguistic anthropology is mainly concerned with the technical analysis of language.

Anthropology - the study of humanity; divisions are physical anthropology, archaeology, ethnology, and anthropological linguistics.

Archaeology - study of material culture.

Art - human endeavor thought to be aesthetic and have meaning beyond simple description. Includes music, dance, sculpture, painting, drawing, stitchery, weaving, poetry, writing, woodworking, etc. A medium of expression where the individual and culture come together.

Assimilation - when one ethnic group absorbs another, so that the cultural traits of the assimilated group become indistinguishable.

Autoethnography - an ethnographic description written by a member of the culture.

Balanced reciprocity - a mode of equal value exchange in which the worth of a good or service and time for its delivery is known.

Band - a small group of related people, who are primarily organized through family bonds. Foraging typifies the subsistence technology. A respected and older person may be looked to for leadership, but the person has no formalized authority.

Big-man - a form of leadership in tribes where the leader achieves power and influence based on ability.

Bilineal - descent in which the individual figures kinship through both the father's and mother's descent group.

Brideprice - an economic exchange by the groom's family to compensate the bride's family upon marriage.

Bureaucracy - government based on a specialized set of offices usually hierarchically organized.

Cannibalism - consuming human flesh. This is reported to occur in the context of warfare, as part of a funeral rite or, rarely, in cases of extreme stress.

Cargo - from the Spanish verb cargar which means to carry and to be in charge of.

Cargo cult - do not confuse "cargo system" with "cargo cult" which is a revitalization movement characterized by the belief that ancestral spirits will bring wanted goods (cargo) and throw off oppressive customs and colonizers.

Cargo system - a set of community offices and obligations a person goes through to achieve recognition and status.

Caste system - the ranking of members in a society by occupational status and degree of purity or pollution as determined by their birth.

Charismatic - the ability to lead and influence large numbers of people.

Chiefdom - political organization is typically inherited through kinship lines. A ranked society in which a few leaders make decisions for the group.

Clan - a noncorporate descent group in which genealogical links to a common ancestor are assumed but are not actually known.

Class stratification - where members of a society are ranked from higher to lower based on wealth, prestige, position, or education.

Colonialism - forced change in which one culture, society, or nation dominates another.

Common interest groups - associations that are formally recognized with a name and social organization, but are not based on age, kinship, marriage, or territory.

Communist: Society works best when each person contributes according to ability and each person receives according to need.

Compasino - an agricultural worker.

Concept - relates facts to propositions and theories. concepts often become variables, but concept is more encompassing. Status and role are concepts. Ranking statuses according to social classes, e.g. lower, middle, and upper, is a variable.

Consanguineal - members of one's kindred who are related by blood line.

Conspicuous consumption - the display of material items for the purpose of impressing others.

Core values - attitudes and beliefs thought to uniquely pattern a culture.

Core-periphery - the structural relation between centralized core, often an urban area, and communities on the periphery, usually tribal or rural, resource-based communities.

Cosmology - ideas about the universe as an ordered system and the place of humans in the universe.

Creole - a person of mixed Spanish and Black African or French and Black African ancestry.

Crimes - violations against the state.

Cross-cousin - children of the opposite-sexed siblings of one's parents, e.g., mother's brother's and father's sister's children.

Cultural anthropology - study of cultural variation and similarities. Includes ethnology and anthropological linguistics. May also include archaeology.

Cultural relativism - understanding the ways of other cultures and not judging these practices according to one's own cultural ways.

Cultural transmission - how culture is passed on through learning from one generation to another. Also referred to as enculturation or socialization.

Culture - The learned patterns of behavior and thought that help a group adapt to it's surroundings.

Culture as an integrated whole - Cultures are systems in which all the parts are related to one another. If one part of the culture changes, this necessitates change in all other related parts.

Culture of discontent - a level of aspirations that far exceeds the bounds of an individual's local opportunities. Also discussed as the gap between expectations and the ability to meet these expectations.

Curer - a specialist who heals with herbal preparations and magic learned through apprenticeships. Curers are usually part-time specialists who are paid for their services and are also called shamans.

Descent group - a kin group whose members are recruited by one of the principles of descent; e.g., matrilineal, patrilineal, etc.

Diffusion - the spread of a cultural pattern from one culture to another, and where no directed change agent is apparent.

Distributive justice - the rules in a culture that specifiy how the economic productivity of that culture is distributed among the members. It is a statement of values about what should be done. e.g.

Divination - obtaining factual knowledge by magical means which have no apparent empirical connection to the information sought.

Division of labor - the division of tasks in a society between women and men, old and young, ability, knowledge, experience.

Domestication - when humans intervene in the breeding patterns of plants or animals.

Dowry - the woman's share of her inheritance from the group of her birth, which is taken with her upon marriage.

Egalitarian - a society without formalized differences in the access to power, influence, and wealth.

Egalitarian: Society works best when everyone has a say in decisions and no person feels they will be injured by choices made by the group.

Emic - an insider's view of a culture.

Enculturation - the process of learning one's own culture, also called socialization.

Endogamy - rules requiring selecting of a marriage partner from within a particular group.

Ethics - the principles of conduct governing an individual or group; concerns for what is right or wrong, good or bad.

Ethnocentrism - judging other cultures by the standards of your own, which you believe to be superior.

Ethnographic novel - an ethnographic description written as a story that may be about an ethnographer's experience or about some event or problem.

Ethnographic present - a description of a culture as it was prior to contact.

Ethnography - description of a culture, usually based on the method of participant observation.

Ethnology - comparative analysis of cultural patterns to explain differences and similarities among societies.

Etic - an outsider's view of a culture.

Evolution - change in the form of a culture. Usually a process of internal cultural change.

Exogamy - rules requiring selection of a marriage partner from outside a particular group.

Extended family - a composite family composed of other relatives besides the nuclear families. Extended families can be constructed across generations by including parent's or children's families or extended laterally by including multiple wives or sibling's families.

Extinction - when a culture dies out. Often the people die out too. Some may become peasants or pass into contemporary society.

Fact - a description of a bit or piece of some domain of inquiry.

Fieldwork - living among a group of people for the purpose of learning about their culture.

Fissioning - a Yanomamo settlement splits due to internal conflict with one group moving away to form a new village.

Folk art - art produced by people not professionally identified as artists.

Foragers - getting food by collecting or hunting what is naturally available. The term used to refer to the subsistence patterns of cultures different from our own continually changes as our values change. Initially, these groups were called "primitives." This term came to be viewed as too ethnocentric since it emphasized they were less developed than "modern" cultures. The term "hunters and gatherers" has been replaced by foragers because of the gender associations with male hunters and female gatherers. Since !Kung women produce 85% of the food by volume, is it appropriate to call them a hunting and gathering society?

Funk - an earthy, unsophisticated style and feeling, or the style and feelings of blues.

Fusion - blending traits from two different cultures to form a new trait. The cargo is a fusion of Mayan and Catholic religious elements. Also called syncretism.

Genealogy - a family tree or web of kinship relationships traced through parents and children. Also called a kindred.

Generalized reciprocity - a mode of exchange in which the time and value of repayment is not specified.

Grammar and syntax - the formal structure of a language and the rules for making sentences and phrases.

Green Revolution - the development of high-yielding varieties of seed for crops such as wheat and rice in Third World countries and requiring extensive technology for planting, irrigation, fertilizing, spraying, and harvesting.

Guru - a Sanskrit and pan-Indian word denoting a spiritual master or teacher. It implies an initiatory relation between master and disciple. The guru passes on oral tradition and ascetic regimen to the student.

Hallmarks of humanity - good and evil, imagination, laughter, love.

Horticulture - an agricultural technology distinguished by the use of hand tools to grow domesticated plants. Does not use draft animals, irrigation, or specially prepared fertilizers.

Humanism - concern for human welfare, dignity and values.

Ideal - what people think the situation should be.

Illness - a malady that is culturally defined.

Imperialism - economic control gained through the corporate organization of nation states.

Industrial society - a society integrated by a complex network of occupational specialties supporting the manufacture of material goods.

Informal economy - the economy common to shanytowns, , slums where goods and services sold or bartered are unregulated by formal institutions.

Information age - a form of culture where electronics joins members of diverse cultural backgrounds together. Greater quantities of information than ever before are available to individuals, yet certainty about the way systems operate is less and more subject to question.

Information society - a society integrated by complex communication networks that rapidly develop and exchange information.

Intensive agriculture - use of irrigation, draft animals, terracing, natural fertilizers, selective breeding, mechanization, etc., to grow more food.

Isolative integration - where a culture tries to prevent another culture from changing its ways and selectively takes from the dominant culture.

Key informants - a few individuals selected on the basis of criteria such as knowledge, compatibility, age, experience, or reputation who provide information about their culture.

Kindred - people related to one another by blood, marriage, and adoption.

Kinesics - body, facial, hand, and arm movements that are used to communicate.

Kinship chart - the diagram of kinship relations using symbols to indicate males, females, marriages, divorces, siblings, descent, and deceased relatives.

Koran - book of teachings for the religion of Islam. Also spelled Quran.

Kula - a set of trade relations among Trobriand men involving the giving away of shell artifacts with the objective of displaying prestige and reinforcing alliances.

Law - the means by which members of a group regulate their conduct and deal with breaches of rules and incompatible interests.

Leveling device - a cultural mechanism which reduces wealth differentials between individuals often by inducing the wealthy to sponsor feasts or to destroy or give away surplus in return for increased prestige.

Libertarian: Society works best when each person is responsible for their own future no matter what happens.

Life cycle - the set of states a person goes through from birth to death.

Lineage - a corporate descent group whose members can trace their genealogical links to a known common ancestor.

Linguistic anthropology - study of how language is used

in various social contexts. Anthropological linguistics focuses more on the interplay of language and culture.

Magic - practices designed to gain control over the supernatural. Magic and religion are separated in several ways in anthropology. For some anthropologists magic tries to gain control over the supernatural. Others see magic as being individual, while religion is a group phenomena that creates lasting social bonds. Malinowski saw magic as a means to an end, while religion was the end in itself. Other anthropologists find separating magic and religion very difficult.

Mandala - artistic representation of the cosmos, a focus for meditation.

Manioc, also called "cassava" - plants grown in the tropics for their starchy, edible rootstock, commonly found as a dietary staple among gardening peoples.

Markets - systems that exchange goods and services using all-purpose money as a standard measure of relative value. Early market systems are characterized by market places or bazaars which are often cyclical, moving among a fixed set of localities, each having its specific market days.

Mational character - studies based on the assumption that collectively members of a society have a distinctive set of psychological qualities. Has been replaced by the concept of core values.

Matriarchy - where a mother figure and women have authority.

Matrilineal - descent traced exclusively through the female line.

Matrilocal - residence after marriage in association with the wife's mother's relatives.

Mediation - dispute settlement through negotiation assisted by an unbiased third party.

Megalopolis - a very large•city or a thickly populated region encompassing one or more large cities.

Melanesia - one of the three principle divisions of Oceania; it includes the islands of the Pacific, Northeast of Australia including New Guinea, Solomon Islands, Vanuatu, New Caledonia, and Fiji. The Melanesian land divers were from the village of Bunlap on Pentecost Island of Vanuatu which under colonial control was called the New Hebrides.

Mestizos - persons of mixed Spanish and Indian cultural background.

Metaphor - application of a word or phrase to an object or concept in order to suggest a comparison.

Micronesia - the small islands of western Oceania.

Modal personality - the personality characteristic held by the most people in the group.

Modernization - the process by which cultures are forced to accept traits from outside.

Moiety - division of a society into two halves based on descent.

Monogamy - marriage in which an individual has one spouse.

Morpheme - the smallest unit of sound that carries a distinct meaning.

Morphology - the study of meaningful units of sound in a language.

Mucrology - the art of etching or painting with a pointed tip of a feathery leaf, etc.

Mulitculturalism - stressing the importance of different cultures, races, and ethnicities.

Nature-nurture - contrasting the biological verses cultural or environmental basis for behavior.

Negative reciprocity - a mode of exchange in which one party has the goal of getting more than is given up.

Negotiation - the use of direct argument and compromise by the parties to a dispute to arrive at a mutually satisfactory agreement.

Neolocal - residence in which the married couple's household has no connection with either the husband's or wife's family.

New World - pertaining to the areas of the world most recently discovered by Europeans; e.g., North and South America.

Noblesse oblige - the obligation of honorable, generous, and responsible behavior associated with high social rank or birth.

Nodes - the individuals in a person's social network.

Nuclear family - a woman and/or husband and dependent children.

Oacification - extending the authority of national government over formerly autonomous people whether by force or persuasion.

Old World - pertaining to areas of the world having the longest period of documented human habitation: e.g., Europe, Asia, and Africa.

Oligarchy - the ruling class. Usually a small group of wealthy individuals.

One-world culture - a popular belief that the future will bring development of a single homogeneous world culture through links created by modern communication, transportation, and trade.

Paralanguage - the use of accent, cadence, pitch, and tone to convey meaning.

Parallel-cousin - children of the same-sexed siblings of one's parents, e.g., mother's sister's and father's brother's children.

Paramount chief - the highest ranking social office in a chiefdom.

Participant observation - living in a culture that is not your own while also keeping a detailed record of your observations and interviews.

Pastoralist - subsistence gained by tending and breeding animals.

Patriarchy - where a father figure and males have authority.

Patrilineal - tracing kinship, inheritance, power through the male line.

Patrilocal - residence after marriage in association with the husband's father's relatives.

Pattern Equality: Society works best when it constantly checks differences in people's well-being and seeks to prevent extreme inequalities.

Peasants - people who produce for their own subsistence in pre-industrial and industrializing state societies—usually rural, lower class, primary producers such as farmers, artisans, or fishermen. They are involved in market relations with urban centers, to which they are also bound politically and administratively.

Peer group - a subgroup of a society in which membership is determined by similar age, sharing the same social status, etc.

Perceived - what people think the situation actually is.

Personality - personal beliefs, expectations, desires, values, and behaviors that derive from the interaction between culture and the individual. Personality is the behaviors and techniques for solving problems that are used by an individual. Personality is to the individual as culture is to the group.

Phoneme - the smallest unit of sound that does not alter the meaning of words in which it occurs.

Phonetics - study of the production, transmission, and reception of sounds in speech.

Phonology - the study of sound patterns in language.

Physical anthropology - study of biological origins and physical variations among human populations.

Pilgrims - those who travel to a shrine or holy place as devotees.

Plurality - when a person wins an election by having the most votes, as opposed to a majority where a person gets more than half of the votes.

Polyandry - a woman has more than one husband.

Polygamy - an individual who has more than one spouse.

Polygyny - a man has more than one wife.

Polynesia - islands in Oceania within the triangle whose corners are the Hawaiian Islands, Easter Island, and New Zealand.

Postmodern - a view that social and cultural reality, as well as social science itself, is a human construction.

Property: Society works best when it protects rights and compensates people, who because of public decisions, lose private opportunities.

Proposition - makes a claim about some domain of inquiry. Also called hypotheses. The higher one's class status, the greater one's power is a proposition.

Protestant work ethic - a value system that stresses the moral value of work, self-discipline, and individual responsibility as the means to improving one's economic well-being.

Rap - a type of rhythmic, rhyming expression spontaneously composed.

Real - what is known to actually be so.

Redistribution - a mechanism whereby a politically or economically powerful individual (or group) collects goods and services from the members of society and reallocates them among the society's members.

Relations - the relationships between individuals in a social network.

Religion - a set of attitudes, beliefs, and practices pertaining to supernatural power.

Revitalization movement - religiously based social movement with the purpose of reforming society.

Ritual - the visible control of abstract thoughts. Tries to control unpredictable events and the supernatural. Tries to know the unknowable and change the unchangeable.

Role - the relation one has with another node in a social network. A loving and affective relationship is the role of being a spouse. See status.

Sacred - things and actions set apart as religious or spiritual which are entitled to reverence.

Science - systematically acquired knowledge that is verifiable.

Seasonal round - the annual pattern followed in the production of food.

Secular - things not regarded as religious or spiritual.

Serial monogamy - a pattern of divorce and monogamous remarriage.

Sex role division of labor - the division of subsistence tasks between women and men.

Shaman - a religious specialist who uses supernatural power in curing. Also called curer or cuerandero.

Shantytown - neighborhoods where poor migrants to cities live. Also called slum, farela, township.

Sister exchange - a shorthand label for a marriage system in which men of different descent groups exchange women who are sometimes their own sisters or daughters and sometimes parallel cousins or the daughters of parallel cousins.

Slash and burn - cultivation with recurrent clearing and burning of vegetation and planting in the burnt fields. Fallow periods for each plot last longer than periods of cultivation. It is sometimes referred to as swidden (or shifting) cultivation.

Social class - people having the same rank in a system that differentiates people from high to low.

Social control - the rules, habits, and customs by which a society tries to maintain order.

Social network - the relationships an individual has with family, friends, co-workers, neighbors, and people in groups to which the person belongs, e.g. church, recreation, political, social, and other groups. See also family, kinship, caste, class.

Social stratification - arranging the members of a society into a pattern of superior and inferior ranks.

Socialist: Society works best when it has a system of social insurance to help people who are disadvantages when unexpected change occurs.

Socialization - the process by which culture is learned; also called enculturation. During socialization individuals internalize a culture's social controls, along with values and norms about right and wrong.

Sociobiology - study of human behavior based on the assumption that human behavior is biologically based.

Sociolinguistics - study of the relationship between language and social factors such as class, ethnicity, age and sex.

Space industrialization - the development of important new manufacturing activities in the environment of outer space.

Specialization - where individuals become experts in producing certain goods or services that are then exchanged.

Spirit cult - a group of adherents to a set of religious beliefs and ritual in which ghosts are believed to interfere in the affairs of the living.

State - a culture that has a formal political organization with a central bureaucracy with the authority to employ legalized force.

Status - the position one has in a social network. The name of a position given to a node. Husband and wife are statuses. See role.

Subsistence - the way by which a culture obtains its food.

Subsistence farmers - when there is very little surplus and nearly all that is produced goes to supporting the farm household.

Supernatural - characteristics of the reality beyond the senses.

Survival of the fittest - a nineteenth century concept that the strongest survive. Often called "Social Darwinism." "Survival of the fittest" misrepresents the process of natural selection. The mechanism of natural selection is reproductive fitness, those who produce offspring. Social Darwinism refers to being the most powerful, which is not the mechanism for natural selection.

Sustainable - being able to continue into the future.

Symbols - physical objects, colors, sounds, movements, scents which convey information through an arbitrary or culturally assigned meaning.

Syncretism - blending traits from two different cultures to form a new trait. Also called fusion.

Terminology systems - the terminology used to refer to cousins. Two-thirds of all world cultures can be classified according to six kinship systems—Hawaiian, Eskimo, Crow, Omaha, Iroquois, Sudanese. The text defines these systems.

Theocracy - a form of state political organization in which the government is based on religious offices.

Theory - several related propositions that explain some domain of inquiry. Also called a school or paradigm.

Third World - countries with economies largely based on agriculture and characterized by low standards of living, high rates of population growth, and general economic and technological dependence upon wealthier industrial nations. A very ethnocentric way of referring to other cultures because it ranks cultures below those of the "First World" like Europe, Japan, Canada, and the

United States.

Torts - violations against an individual.

Tribe - a group that centers around kinship units and common-interest groups that cross-cut kindred boundaries. Horticulture typifies the subsistence technology. People who attain prestige according to cultural standards may be seen as leaders. The big-man institution is quite common in tribes.

Urbanization - the process by which more and more people come to live in cities.

Utilitarian: Society works best when the majority chooses what will produce the greatest good for the greatest number of people.

Warfare - organized, armed conflict between groups, each of which is motivated by a common purpose.

World view - the beliefs about the limits and workings of the world shared by the members of a society and represented in their myths, lore, ceremonies, social conduct, and gėneral values.

BIBLIOGRAPHY

A. Van Exem (1991): *"The Mistake, reviewed after a century"*, *Sevartham* 1991.

Aoki, Haruo. "Nez Perce Texts." *University of California Publications in Linguistics* 90 (1979).

Arbib, Michael A. (1989) *The Metaphorical Brain 2: Neural Networks and Beyond*. New York: Wiley.

Asad, Talal, ed. (1973) *Anthropology & the Colonial Encounter*. Atlantic Highlands, NJ: Humanities Press.

Barley, Nigel (1983) *The innocent anthropologist: notes from a mud hut*. London: British Museum Publications.

Barth, Fredrik, Andre Gingrich, Robert Parkin, and Sydel Silverman. 2005. *One Discipline, Four Ways: British, German, French, and American anthropology*. Chicago: University of Chicago Press.

Bass, W M. 2005. *Human Osteology: A Laboratory and Field Manual*. 5th Edition. Columbia: Missouri Archaeological Society.

Beavert, Virginia. *The Way it Was: Anuku Iwacha: Yakima Legends*.Yakima: Franklin Press, 1974.

Boyd, Robert. *People of The Dalles: the Indians of Wascopam Mission*. 1996. Reprint. Lincoln: University of Nebraska Press, 2004.

Buikstra, J. E and Ubelaker, D. H. (eds.) 1994. *Standards for Data Collection from Human Skeletal Remains.*

Arkansas Archeological Survey Research Series No. 44.

Calvin, William H. (1989) *The Cerebral Symp*hony. New York: Bantam.

Christine A. Hastorf (Editor), Virginia S. Popper (Editor), *Current Paleoethnobotany : Analytical Methods and Cultural Interpretations of Archaeological Plant Remains (Prehistoric Archeology and Ecology series)*, University of Chicago Press (January 15, 1989).

Clifford, James and George E. Marcus (1986) *Writing culture: the poetics and politics of ethnography*. Berkeley: University of California Press.

Cox, M and Mays, S. (eds.) 2000. *Human Osteology in Archaeology and Forensic Science*. London: Greenwich Medical Media.

Curtis, Edward. *The North American Indian. Vol. 8, Chinookans and Nez Perce*. Norwood, MA: Plimpton Press, 1911. Reprint. New York: Johnson Reprint, 1970.

D'Andrade, R. "The Sad Story of Anthropology: 1950-1999." In E. L. Cerroni-Long, ed. *Anthropological Theory in North America*. Westport: Berin & Garvey 1999. download

Daniel L. Migliore, *Faith Seeking Understanding: An Introduction to Christian Theology* (Grand Rapids: Eerdmans, 2004)

Darnell, Regna. (2001) *Invisible Genealogies: A History of Americanist Anthropology*. Lincoln, NE: University of Nebraska Press.

David Burrell, *Freedom and Creation in Three Traditions* (Notre Dame: University of Notre Dame Press, 1994)

Deeb, Benjamin. (2007) *Anthropology and Social Problems: A Manual of Change*.

Donald, Merlin (1991) *Origins of the Modern Mind: Three Stages in the Evolution of Culture and Cognition*. Cambridge, MA: Harvard University Press.

Duncan Dormor et al (eds), *Anglicanism, the Answer to Modernity* (London: Continuum, 2003).

Falconer, D. S. & Mackay TFC (1996). Introduction to Quantitative Genetics. Fourth edition. Addison Wesley Longman, Harlow, Essex, UK.

Falk, Dean (1992) *Braindance*. New York: Henry Holt & Co.

Franchere, Gabriel. *Journal of a Voyage on the North West Coast of North America during the years 1811, 1812, 1813 and 1814*. Translated by W. Kaye and Wessie Lamb. Publications of the Champlain Society 45: 1969.

Geertz, Clifford (1973) *The Interpretation of Cultures*. New York: Basic Books.

Geertz, Clifford (1995) *After the fact: two countries, four decades, one anthropologist*. Cambridge, MA: Harvard University Press.

Gibbs, George. *Tribes of Western Washington and Northwest Oregon*. Reprint. Seattle: Shorey Book Store: 1970. (First published as "Tribes of Western Washington and Northwest Oregon." *Contributions to North American Ethnology* 1, 1877: 157-241.

Gray, Dennis. "The Takelma and their Athapascan Neighbors." *University of Oregon Anthropological Papers* 37 (1987).

Harper, J. Russell, ed. *Paul Kane's Frontier*. Austin: University of Texas Press: 1971.

Harris, Marvin. (2001[1968]) *The rise of anthropological theory: a history of theories of culture*. AltaMira Press. Walnut Creek, CA.

Heuze, Gérard: Où Va l'Inde Moderne? L'Harmattan, Paris 1993 A. Tirkey: "Evangelization among the Uraons", Indian Missiological Review, June 1997, esp. p. 30-32. Elst 2001

Hugh of St. Victor, *Commentariorum in Hierarchiam Coelestem*, Expositio to Book 9: 'theologia, id est, divina Scriptura' (in Migne's *Patrologia Latina* vol.175, 1091C).

Hunn, Eugene. *N'chi-Wana (the "Big River)*. Seattle: University of Washington Press, 1990.

Jacobs, Melville. "Kalapuya Texts." *University of Washington Publications in Anthropology* 11 (1945).

Jacobs, Melville. 1958-59. *Clackamas Chinook Texts*. 2 vols. Bloomington: University of Indiana Press.

Jerison, H.J. and I. Jerison (1988) *Intelligence and Evolutionary Biology*. Berlin: Springer-Verlag.

John Shelby Spong, *Why Christianity Must Change or Die* (New York: Harper Collins, 2001)

Jose Ignacio Cabezon, 'Buddhist Theology in the Academy' in Roger Jackson and John J. Makransky's *Buddhist Theology: Critical Reflections by Contemporary Buddhist Scholars* (London: Routledge, 1999), pp.25-52.

Josephy, Alvin. *The Nez Perce Indians and the Opening of the Northwest*. New Haven: Yale University Press, 1965. Reprint. Boston: Houghton Mifflin, 1997.

Kautilya: *The Arthashastra* 9:2:13-20, Penguin edition, p. 685.

Kehoe, Alice B. (1998) *The Land of Prehistory: A Critical History of American Archaeology*.

Kristen J. Gremillion, *People, Plants, and Landscapes: Studies in Paleoethnobotany*, University of Alabama Press (February 1, 1997).

L. Gardet, 'Ilm al-kalam' in *The Encyclopedia of Islam*, ed. P.J. Bearman et al (Leiden: Koninklijke Brill NV, 1999).

Laughlin, C.D., John McManus and E.G. d'Aquili (1990) *Brain, Symbol and Experience: Toward a Neurophenomenology of Human Consciousness*. New York: Columbia University Press.

Lee, Daniel and Joseph Frost. *Ten Years in Oregon. 1844.* Reprint. Fairfield, WA: Ye Galleon Press: 1968.

Lévi-Strauss, Claude (1967) *Tristes tropiques*. Translated from the French by John Russell. New York: Atheneum.

Lewis, Herbert S. (1998) "The Misrepresentation of Anthropology and its Consequences." *American Anthropologist*, 100: 716-731.

Lewis, Herbert S. (2004) "Imagining Anthropology's History." *Reviews in Anthropology*, v. 33.

Lewis, Herbert S. (2005) "Anthropology, the Cold War, and Intellectual History. In R. Darnell & F.W. Gleach, eds. *Histories of Anthropology Annual*, Vol. I.

Lewis, Meriwether, and William Clark. *The Journals of the Lewis & Clark Expedition. Vols. 5-7.* Edited by Gary Moulton. Lincoln: University of Nebraska Press, 1988-91.

Lynch M & Walsh B (1998). Genetics and Analysis of Quantitative Traits. Sinauer, Sunderland, MA.

Malinowski, Bronis³aw (1967) *A diary in the strict sense of the term*. Translated by Norbert Guterman. New York, Harcourt, Brace & World.

Michael S. Kogan, 'Toward a Jewish Theology of Christianity' in *The Journal of Ecumenical Studies* 32.1 (Winter 1995), 89-106; available online at

Pearsall, Deborah M, *Paleoethnobotany: A Handbook of*

Procedures, Second Edition, Academic Press, San Diego (2000).

Pels, Peter & Oscar Salemink, eds. (2000) *Colonial Subjects: Essays on the Practical History of Anthropology*.

Peter Abelard's *Theologia Christiana*, and - perhaps most famously, of Thomas Aquinas' *Summa Theologica*

Price, David. (2004) *Threatening Anthropology: McCarthyism and the FBI's Surveillance of Activist Anthropologists*.

Rabinow, Paul. (1977) *Reflections on Fieldwork in Morocco*.

Ray, Verne. "Lower Chinook Ethnographic Notes" *University of Washington Publications in Anthropology* 7(2) (1938): 29-165.

Roff DA (1997). Evolutionary Quantitative Genetics. Chapman & Hall, New York.

Ross, Alexander. *Adventures of the First Settlers on the Oregon or Columbia River*. 1849. Reprint. Corvallis: Oregon State University Press. 2000.

Ruby, Robert. *The Cayuse: Imperial Tribesmen of Old Oregon*. Norman: University of Oklahoma Press, 1972.

Ruby, Robert. *The Chinook Indians: Traders of the Lower Columbia*. 1976. Reprint. Norman: University of Oklahoma Press, 1988.

Salzmann, Zdenìk. (1993) *Language, culture, and society: an introduction to linguistic anthropology*. Boulder, CO: Westview Press.

Sapir, Edward. "Takelma Texts." *University of Pennsylvania Anthropological Publications* 2(1) (1909): 1-267.

Sapir, Edward. "Wishram Texts." *Publications of the American Ethnological Society* 2 (1909).

Shweder, Richard A., and Robert A. LeVine, eds. (1984)

Culture Theory: essays on mind, self, and emotion. Cambridge, UK: Cambridge University Press.

Spier, Leslie and Edward Sapir. "Wishram Ethnography." *University of Washington Publications in Anthropology* 3(3) (1930): 150-300.

Spier, Leslie. *Klamath Ethnography*. Reprint. New York: Krause Reprint, 1976. (First published as "Klamath Ethnography." *University of California Publications in Archaeology and Ethnology* 30 (1930).)

Spinden, Herbert. *Nez Perce Indians*. Reprint. New York: Krause Reprint, 1964. (First published as "Nez Perce Indians." *Memoirs of the American Anthropological Association* 2(3) (1908).)

Stern, Theodore. *Indian Relations at Fort Nez Perces. Vol. 1, Chiefs and Chief Traders.*

Corvallis: Oregon State University Press, 1993.

Stocking, George, Jr. (1968) *Race, Culture and Evolution.* New York: Free Press.

Strong, Emory. *Stone Age on the Columbia*. 1959. Reprint. Portland, Ore.: Binfords & Mort: 1967.

Suttles, Wayne. *Northwest Coast. Vol. 7, Handbook of North American Indians*. Washington: Smithsonian Institution Press: 1990.

Swan, James. *The Northwest Coast; or Three Years Residence in Washington Territory*. 1857. Reprint. Seattle: University of Washington Press, 1972.

Timothy Gorringe, *Crime*, Changing Society and the Churches Series (London:SPCK, 2004)

Trencher, Susan. (2000) *Mirrored Images: American Anthropology and American Culture, 1960-1980.*

Tripathy, B. (1973), *A Portrait of Population, Orissa,* Census of India, Series 16, Orissa Govt. Press, Cuttack.

Vidyarth, L.P. (1975), "Strategy for Tribal Development in India," *Proceeding of the Seminar on Tribal Development,* Bhubaneswar.

Walker, Deward (1998). *Handbook of North American Indians. Vol. 2, Plateau.* Washington: Smithsonian Institution Press.

Winkelman, Michael (2000), *Shamanism: The Neural Ecology of Consciousness and Healing*. Westport, CT: Bergin & Garvey.

INDEX

C

D

E

S

T

U

V

W

Y

Z

■■■